CLEA

CLEAN *Hands*

1996 KESWICK MINISTRY

OM
publishing

First published 1996 by OM Publishing

02 01 00 99 98 97 96   7 6 5 4 3 2 1

OM Publishing is an imprint of Paternoster Publishing,
P.O. Box 300, Carlisle, Cumbria, CA3 0QS, UK.

British Library Cataloguing in Publication Data

A catalogue record for this book is available from
the British Library

ISBN 1–85078–256–3

Typeset by Photoprint, Torquay, Devon
and printed in the UK by Cox & Wyman Ltd., Reading

CONTENTS

'Clean Hands'

INTRODUCTION BY THE CHAIRMAN OF THE 1996 CONVENTION

Holiness, in terms of practical godliness of life, has from the first been the pervading theme of the Keswick Convention, and its presentation to the thousands attending has always been undergirded by the earnest prayer that all of us may be deepened in our Christian lives, and that this will be seen in the sheer quality of godliness pervading our lives by God's grace as we respond to the preaching.

Summer 1996 therefore presented the very clear challenge to give to the Lord 'clean hands', which, as Psalm 24:4 implies, result from 'a pure heart'. It was a blessed fortnight and the ministry was rich indeed, carrying with it again and again the challenge to apply the truth to our own lives. In one sense it was also challenging because we were made to think; both sets of Bible Readings gave no easy answers, but laid out the ground and left us to think the issues through. This was particularly true of Stuart Briscoe's expositions of the Ten Commandments, raising issue after issue and refusing to do our homework for us!

These brief pages can of course make no reference to many facets of the Convention week: for example the hundreds of children and their Scripture Union friends, and the thrillingly blessed work among teenagers. Nor can the many excellent and relevant seminars be included. When you read the address on Caleb, offer a prayer for the more than 120 men and women of all ages who dedicated their lives to serve God wherever and whenever He will call—and listen prayerfully, because that call may be God's word to you too.

And no abbreviated summary of the addresses can do full justice to the ministry, though we are indeed indebted to those who have worked so hard to present these pages to us, especially David and Tricia Porter. Audio and video tapes are of course available, and details are given at the end of the book.

We were blessed with the most beautiful summer sunshine in one of the most beautiful parts of these favoured islands, and the fellowship was rich. But all that is secondary to the main purpose of the Convention, that every one of us should come away deepened in our love for the Lord and strengthened in our commitment to serve His people with pure hearts and clean hands in today's most challenging world.

May God bless these pages to all who read them.

Keith A. A. Weston
Chairman of the Keswick Convention Council

EDITOR'S INTRODUCTION

For some years now the Keswick Book, which used be transcribed from tapes by a stalwart army of typists and then edited
and abridged by myself, has been a husband-and-wife operation:
Tricia has expertly transcribed over 100,000 words of Keswick
Ministry this summer, and I would like to acknowledge her
major contribution to the book you are reading.

Regular readers will find no surprises in this introduction. As
in previous years, the speakers have graciously waived the right
to check the edited text, which has as always been read through
carefully on their behalf by a representative of the Keswick
Council. This is the only way to get the book in the shops as
quickly as we do.

The material is abridged, and if you want the full text you
must make use of the excellent tape and video libraries mentioned on p.000. This will also give you the opportunity to hear
the speakers' own voices, which can only ever be captured to a
limited extent on the printed page. For example Rev. Stuart
Briscoe's warmth and immaculate timing of humorous anec-
dotes have been impossible to preserve on paper, and some of the
knottier passages in Romans gain immeasurably by the clarity of
Rev. Michael Wilcock's spoken delivery. On the other hand,
none of the content, and no reference to Scripture, has been
omitted, though as always you will find this book most rewarding
if you read it with an open Bible in front of you.

Following Keswick tradition, pronouns referring to Deity are
capitalised, but in quotations—including biblical quotations—
we follow the style of the quoted text. As no Bible version

capitalises pronouns, this is a useful way of detecting if a speaker is paraphrasing—the pronouns will be capitalised if he is.

I have had my usual enjoyable hunt to check references to quoted works, which this year has taken me to well-loved older hymnbooks, the works of Shakespeare, and a painting in Liverpool that Dr Steve Brady and myself know well. The brevity of the editorial schedule means that some of the more obscure references have been left for you, the readers, to identify for your own satisfaction.

David Porter

THE BIBLE READINGS

'The Practice of Holiness'
Romans 12–16

by Rev. Michael Wilcock

1 : The Life We Are To Live
Romans 12:1–21

It is the constant challenge to preachers, and the constant cry of those who are preached at, that preaching should be practical. And you can't get more practical than Romans 12 onwards! I find it very striking that one of the most profound parts of all Scripture, Romans 1–11, leads straight into one of the most practical parts, Romans 12–16.

We could take chapter 12 as it stands, and I think we would find it very challenging to work through the commands and exhortations that come from God through the mouth of His servant Paul. They comprise a very wide-ranging series of exhortations to Christian living. We would find that they all have to do with practicalities: 'the practice of holiness', to use the overall title of these five Bible readings. In one way or the other, the practicalities of Romans 12 would apply to every one of us.

But I want instead to set the whole chapter in its context, so that we can hear more clearly what the Holy Spirit is saying to us when later we read the chapter for ourselves on our own.

I want to focus chiefly on the opening two verses under the headings of three important words; and I trust this will help us to grasp what practical holy living is. The three words are 'theology' (the first half of verse 1); 'worship' (the second half of verse 1); and 'sanctification' (verse 2).

Theology (12:1a)

'Therefore, I urge you, brothers, in view of God's mercy, to offer your bodies as living sacrifices, holy and pleasing to God. . .'

Theology is the soil where practical holy living grows. The practice of holiness is not a florist's shop but a garden where flowers grow. You don't buy bunches of cut flowers and pretend that's a Christian life. It is a living, growing thing, and the necessary soil for the growth of Christian holy living is theology; concerning which I think there are three points in these early verses of Romans 12.

The composition of the soil

First the very first word that Paul writes: 'Therefore'. It's a word Paul uses frequently in his letters. He links one thing to another: he talks theology first, says 'therefore', and goes on to talk Christian practice. 'I want you to live in a certain way because of what I've just been saying to you by way of theological truth. The theology is the soil in which I want practical holy Christian living to grow.' So what came before the 'therefore'? I believe that the reference is to everything that Paul has so far written to the Romans, eleven whole chapters of the most extraordinary theology. 'In view of all that you've learnt so far, I want you to live a holy life.'

Bishop Handley C. G. Moule was Bishop of Durham in the early part of this century (and a great Keswick man, I believe). He wrote a book on Romans in which he imagines the apostle Paul sitting in the house of Gaius in Corinth, mulling over the letter that Tertius his secretary has just finished writing out for him. And he sees this astonishing gospel, whose glorious line and argument he has been caused to draw as it was never drawn before, on those papyrus pages. The truth of God, not of man, veiled so long, promised so long, known at last, the gospel which displays the sinner's peace, the believer's life, the radiant boundless future of the saints, and in all and above all the eternal love of the Father and the Son! Romans 1–11 is a grand comprehensive theology, the sum of the whole of the Scriptures' teaching on the subject of who God is, what man is and of the dealings of one with the other. That is the theology which lies behind the word 'therefore', on the basis of which Paul urges us to practise holy living. And it is vital that every Christian who takes his or her faith seriously should have the grasp of Christian truth which leads to that 'therefore'; the grand summary of Christian theology, of which the soil is made in which holy living is to grow.

Those of us who are in the ministry know from hard experience that our ministry depends on it. You can't practise our sort of practical Christian living without it. Charles Spurgeon said, 'I don't know how my soul would have been kept alive if it had not have been for the searching of Scripture which preaching has involved.' It's an enormous privilege, for those of us who are in the ministry of the word, to be forced back again and again into that theological soil. It is there, if anything is to grow, we have to put down our roots.

Likewise those not in the ministry but with a Christian background and upbringing know it too. Maybe, with me, you recognise what a precious thing it was to be brought up from our mother's knee to know the things of Scripture and the things of God. We never called it theology then, but that's what it was. The soil was being prepared.

The balance of the soil

Therefore, 'in view of God's mercy'—those eleven chapters of theology—live this way. You could sum up all that theology in that one little phrase. And it tells us something about the balance of the soil. Many theologies in the Christian world are unbalanced; they put other things at the centre, they reckon other things to be the vital element in the soil. But if all the ingredients are properly balanced, this is the vital element. If, when you say, 'It is because of the theology of Romans 1–11 that I am encouraged to live a Christian life', you mean the mercies of God, then you've got the balance right.

The whole vast complex scheme of Christian theology is centrally about this one thing: Romans 1:11, climaxing in that amazing doxology in 11:33–36.

> Oh, the depth of the riches of the wisdom and
>   knowledge of God!
> How unsearchable his judgments,
>   and his paths beyond tracing out!

What lies behind that and sparks off Paul's paean of praise? Look at the verses that immediately precede it: 'Just as you who were at one time disobedient to God have now received mercy as a result of their disobedience, so they too have now become disobedient in order that they too may now receive mercy as a result of God's mercy to you. For God has bound all men over to disobedience so that he may have mercy on them all' (Rom. 11:30–32)

Oh, the depth of the wisdom and riches of God! That's what it's all about. Jesus, as so often in His stories, put it very simply. Two men were praying in the temple. The Pharisee thanked God for all that he himself was, and the publican said, 'God be merciful to me, a sinner' (cf Luke 18). If you start there and stay there, then however grand may be your grasp of theology you will have the balance right and you will understand what Romans 1–11 is really about. Of course it's true that the more theology you know the better, but I must tell you that the quantity and diversity of your theological knowledge are far less important than its balance. Our knowledge of God and His ways with mankind are not intended to be primarily extensive, but intensive. What you don't know yet doesn't matter, so long as you go back again and again to this grand central truth. Whatever else you add around the edges and however wide your knowledge becomes, as long as you can say the heart of the gospel is God's mercy to the sinner, then the balance is right. And everything else you learn—if it has to do with God who in His mercy set up the great plan of salvation centred on the cross of His Son, the Lord Jesus Christ, and by that plan rescues and transforms the undeserving—will fit in around it.

The use of the soil
This focus on God's mercy leads us to one more point about theology as the soil of practical holy living. In verse 3 you will see

that we are to think about ourselves 'in accordance with the measure of faith God has given you'; and at the end of verse 6 Paul says, 'If a man's gift is prophesying, let him use it in proportion to his faith.' Faith is here a measure, a standard. I think that many Christians, when they read those words in the NIV 'the measure of faith' and 'in proportion to his faith' conclude that Paul is talking about the quantity of faith; that some advanced Christians have a lot of it and some don't have very much. (And that some have been Christians a long time and still don't have very much, while others are new converts and have a great deal of faith.) But I do not believe that is Paul's meaning here. He is not talking about something that puts Christians in some kind of ranking system, but about something that puts Christians on an equal level; about a sense in which they are all alike.

There is much debate among commentators about the little phrase in verse 3, 'the measure of faith'. Charles Cranfield, that dear man who was at Durham when I was a student forty-five years ago and still adorns the Durham scene, produced one of the finest commentaries ever written on Romans. He points out that the Greek word for 'faith' can have five different meanings, the Greek word for 'measure' can have seven different meanings, and even the little word 'of' can have two different meanings. If you multiply them all together, there are seventy different ways you can understand this phrase.

I'll tell you which I think is the right one. I believe that Paul is saying something like this: 'Think of yourself with sober judgement as God has given each of you faith as a measure.' The measure is faith. And in verse 6, 'If a man's gift is prophesying, let him use it'—not 'in proportion to his faith', but 'with faith as a standard'. He is talking about faith in a certain sense, to be used as a measure when you consider what God wants you to do with the gifts He's given to you. It is meant to be a standard of reference when you talk to God about how your Christian life is developing. Paul, I believe, is urging us to go back to the beginnings of our Christian experience and to that original faith we had when we first came to God through Christ, realised that we were undeserving sinners, and cast ourselves upon His mercy. We are back in Luke 18; this is the faith with which the publican said, 'God, have mercy on me, a sinner' (Luke 18:13).

Handley Moule got it right a hundred years ago. 'Let the Christian's use of every gift follow the proportion of his faith.' That's to say, let it be true to his entire dependence on the revealed Christ. So that when God opens up for you or for me, maybe after we've been Christians for many years, a new opportunity or gift we didn't realise we had, something new, the next step in our Christian life—and he says, 'I urge you to go back to that original wide-eyed, wondering, innocent faith which says, "God has given this to me? Why to me? I'm just a sinner, I have nothing, Lord thank You, I cast myself back on You and accept it as a free gift to an undeserving sinner".'—use that faith as a measure, as a standard for every new experience that comes your way as you seek to follow the practice of holy living. It is by that yardstick that we are to measure every subsequent experience, development, gift and service. It has to do with every stage in the growth of practical holy living.

Glance quickly down the rest of chapter 12, and notice in verses 3–8 all the gifts that God has given to us. See in verses 9–13 all the experiences that come the way of the Christian. See in verses 14–16 all the relationships spoken of there. And see in verses 17–21 all the problems that may come our way. Paul is saying, 'As you confront each of these new things, come to it as the original, undeserving but believing sinner, putting your trust in Jesus.' That entire dependence on your Saviour, again—that's how the soil is to be used.

We go back to that grand theology and we see at its heart the mercy of God. However far on we may be in the Christian life or in Christian service, with each new day we say, 'Lord, I am in a sense back where I started. I want You to cleanse me again. Give me a vision again. I am still a sinner, You are still a Saviour. Everything I have received until now and what I am now receiving is a gift from You to an undeserving sinner. Thank You, Lord. I trust You for the coming day as I have trusted You for all the days gone by.' That is how theology becomes the soil in which practical holy living is to grow.

Worship (12:1b)

Worship is the definition of what practical holy living is. How would you define worship?

One suggestion might be, 'It's what happens in my church three times every Sunday.'

'No, no, no,' somebody else would say, 'I came to a meeting in your church and we had some preaching and prayers but there wasn't any worship. We didn't do any singing, that's why there wasn't any worship.'

'No, no, *no*,' says somebody else. 'That's not what I call worship. You can have a service with all kinds of singing, psalms and funny old traditional hymns, but there wouldn't be any worship in it unless you sang *a particular type of song*. That's my definition of worship.'

These definitions of worship are progressively narrower. But the definition of worship ought to go in the opposite direction; it should become broader. Worship is defined by practical, holy living. Paul gives us that definition in verse 1: 'Therefore, I urge you, brothers, in view of God's mercy, to offer your bodies as living sacrifices, holy and pleasing to God—this is your spiritual act of worship'—or instead of 'spiritual' I will substitute the word 'intelligent'. You may think this rather an odd change, but I will explain shortly. First I want to say something about worship.

Worship is sacrifice

We're told here that worship is the offering of our bodies as a sacrifice to God, which is another way of saying 'practical holy Christian living'. I used to read this verse with the emphasis on the word 'sacrifice' because the notion of religion which included sacrifices, in which people brought animals to be slaughtered in a holy place, is very alien to us. That's not we mean by religion, generally speaking, in our modern world, and certainly not in this Western, Christianised world. We can easily forget that in the world of the New Testament 2,000 years ago, sacrifice was commonplace. On a particular holy day you went to some temple or pagan holy place, and you took an offering to the holy person or priest. It might well have been a living creature, an animal or bird, which was duly slaughtered.

Everybody took it for granted that that was what religion was. And when Paul's readers came to Romans 12:1, I am quite sure that they would not have said, 'Christianity says, you are to offer your bodies as a *sacrifice*? Is that what religion is all about?' Quite the opposite. They would have read it like this: 'Christianity requires you to offer *your bodies* as a sacrifice. Any old Tom, Dick, or Harry going to the pagan temple offers a sacrifice. But Christianity says you are to offer your bodies as a sacrifice, and that's the difference.'

That's the arresting thing about Romans 12:1, and it is one of the differences between Christianity and all other religions. Most offer sacrifices, but the Christian faith holds that what you offer as a sacrifice is your body. These bodies that get up in the morning and yawn and wash and dress (and some of them shave), that go downstairs and snap at the kids over breakfast, that confront a mountain of work in the course of the day, that walk down the street and chat to the neighbours—these bodies of ours are what we are to offer as our religion; our ordinary everyday lives, the lives we lead with these minds and limbs. That is a great distinctive about the Christian faith.

Intelligent worship

You may have other translations which suggest 'spiritual', 'reasonable', 'rational' or even 'logical worship'. But on the whole I prefer the word 'intelligent', because Paul is talking about the worship of people who know what they are doing, who are not thoughtless, mindless worshippers. They have given some attention to this question and they know what Christian worship really means. They've read Romans 12:1 and they realise that true Christian worship is the definition of what practical holy living is. And they know that this is what God means by the word worship.

Most of the choruses I sing in most of my church meetings are worshipful. They are part of worship. But they are not in themselves worship and should not be defined as worship. Even if I broaden my terms and include traditional hymns, metrical psalms and even Anglican psalms, I'm still not talking about worship as such. And even if I include everything that is going on in my church building on a Sunday and talk about Sunday services—what I do in St Nicholas', Durham does not of itself constitute worship.

It is easy to make parallels between what the Old Testament shows us about the religion of ancient Israel and what was then thought of as worship, and our own world; presumably the equivalent of the Jewish temple is the Christian church, the equivalents of the rites and ceremonies in ancient times in Jerusalem are the services that happen in our churches today, and the equivalent of the Jewish priesthood is the present ministry of the church. But to identify connections like that is wrong. These things are not equivalent. That was the religion of the Jews and it has a different equivalent now.

That does not mean at all that we should not get together on Sundays and use the church buildings we've inherited or perhaps built ourselves to gather to sing God's praises. That is part of what Christians are expected to do. We come together to pray, to hear God's word, to encourage one another; all that is provided for in the New Testament. But it is not the equivalent of Old Testament Jewish priestly worship, all of which has been summed up and transmuted into something wonderful and new.

'Therefore, I urge you, brothers, in view of God's mercy, to offer your bodies as living sacrifices, holy and pleasing to God. . .' That is your intelligent worship, and Christians who know what they are doing know that. I know that when I go down to St Nicholas', Durham at the foot of the hill on a Sunday morning, that will be part of my worship. I also know that the walk down the hill and the walk back up again is worship. And when some of us sit down and have minced preacher for lunch, that too is worship. And not only what we do on Sundays, but what we do on Monday mornings is worship. When we go to work, that is worship—all these things are worship. When I have a day off, that is worship as well.

Worship is not simply what you find in verses 6 and 7: 'If a man's gift is prophesying, let him use it in proportion to his

faith. If it is serving, let him serve; if it is teaching, let him teach.'
Worship is also verse 8: 'If it is encouraging, let him encourage;
if it is contributing to the needs of others'—all these things are
included in the definition of worship. This is the intelligent
worship of people who know what worship is, and their notion of
it is in line with God's notion. Interestingly, J. B. Phillips used
the phrase 'intelligent worship' fifty years ago in *Letters to Young
Churches* (1947), though I would have to take issue with his
phrase, 'I beg you, my brothers, as an act of intelligent worship'.
This misses the point. It is not an 'act' of worship. The whole of
our lives is to be a process of intelligent worship.

Theological colleges offering courses on 'worship' often really
mean courses in liturgy. But liturgy is not what we are talking
about here. The ancient story about the family who inscribed
above the kitchen sink the words 'Divine worship conducted
here three times daily' is not just whimsical. That family had got
hold of a very important truth. They could have inscribed the
words in many other places, they might taken it with them in
their briefcases or handbags: 'Divine worship is conducted here
constantly.'

As Horatius Bonar wrote,

> Fill Thou my life, O Lord my God,
> In every part with praise,
> That my whole being may proclaim
> Thy being and Thy ways . . .
> Praise in the common things in life,
> Its goings out and in;
> Praise in each duty and each deed,
> However small and mean.

That, as Romans 12:1 tells us, is what praise and worship
really is.

Sanctification (12:2)

Finally, sanctification; the process by which practical holy living
develops.

Verse 2: 'Do not conform any longer'—or, as it should be, 'do not be conformed any longer'—'to the pattern of this world, but be transformed by the renewing of your mind. Then you will be able to test and approve what God's will is—his good, pleasing and perfect will.' We see here what holiness, the sanctified life, is; and how it happens.

I want to talk to about grammar. 'What a dull subject!' you say. I have to tell you that it is still eminently practical. This perhaps is the most practical part of all in practical, holy living. I'm talking about the two verbs that Paul uses here: 'do not be conformed, but be transformed'. Those verbs are in the passive voice, the imperative mood and the present tense. I'll tell you what they mean.

Two passive verbs

Firstly, Paul is using two verbs in the passive voice. That is to say, he is talking about something that is being done to you: 'being conformed', 'being transformed'. A force independent of you is trying to conform you to this world; another force is aiming to transform you by the renewing of your mind. Two verbs in the passive voice. The world is aiming to conform you to itself, and all the new nature which God by His Holy Spirit has implanted in you is aiming to transform you.

In the 1930s Gladys Aylward went all on her own, without the backing of any organisation, to China to serve God. Her biography is a thrilling, inspiring story of things that the Holy Spirit of God did through her—those are the terms her biographer uses. But I wonder whether she ever realised how powerful an acted parable one incident in her life was. She obtained a paid job with the Chinese government as a local civil servant; the local mandarin appointed her as a foot inspector. Although in those days the old China was giving way to the new, women of every age still tottered around on tiny, deformed feet that had been tightly bound when they were babies, so that they would never develop normally. It was extremely painful and degrading But the new Chinese government of the 1930s was out to abolish this bad old custom. Who would implement that policy? The 'foreign devil' was chosen to do it. She was the one who had the entrée. She travelled on a donkey from village to village in the Chinese mountains, enforcing the unbinding.

What she was doing was a parable of her call to China. Here were the bands of a bad old worldly fashion, which were cramping these little creatures. They were not growing up as God meant them to be and it was her enormous privilege to have those restricting bands taken off, so that the girls could grow up with their feet as God intended. The power of the world around was signified by those bands. It was a culture in which that deformity was accepted, in which most people thought nothing of it. The custom was unquestioned. It was the world around, squeezing them literally into its own mould.

That's J. B. Phillips again, of course. It's his wonderful, memorable translation of verse 2: 'Don't let the world around you squeeze you into its own mould, but let God re-mould your minds from within.' And as the little feet were released, the power that was within that little body began to make the foot grow again as God intended it to grow. There was an inner power.

That is what Paul is saying. It's the passive voice of both verbs: 'Don't let the world around you squeeze you into its own mould. . . There is a power around you that will conform you if you let it. But instead, be transformed. There is a power inside you which will renew you if you let it.'

Two imperative verbs

Both verbs are commands. That's a strange paradox, isn't it? A force outside us, or inside us, is doing something to us, and yet at the same time we are told to do something about it. Therein is a great and profound theological mystery which I won't explore now—except to say that here is the command to you and to me to stop letting one thing happen to us and to make sure that another thing happens to us. The command is, 'Be transformed by the renewing of your mind.' What is that renewing of the mind?

I would want to say that it is a conscious development. It is something that we are commanded to do and therefore we can do, and therefore we take thought and effort to do it. It is the conscious thought that says, 'Today I must quite deliberately and consciously size up every situation that I find myself entering upon, to assess and discern it according to what the Spirit has told me in the word of God, to discern what is happening in the world around me and make decisions accordingly. I must personally decide in obedience to these commands, to say 'no' to the bands of the world which are trying to force me into an alien shape, and to say 'yes' to the power of the Spirit who wants to make me more like Christ.

That is the command, and I am to obey it deliberately day by day. I am to reject this thing, to embrace that thing, so that gradually day by day I shall become ever less like the world's shape and ever more like Christ's shape. That is the process of sanctification.

Two verbs in the present tense

These words are happening now. What's more, they are going on happening. The Greek actually says, 'Stop the process of being conformed to this world, and carry on with the process of being transformed by the renewing of your minds.' This is something which will be happening continuously. The present tense tells us that sanctification is the process by which practical holy living develops.

A three-year old child in a mountain village in China; a little girl, a toddler, under the (literally) continuous pressure from the world to conform to its fashion. It went on day after agonising day, until those feet ceased to feel the pain, they became so accustomed to it. But at the same time, at any rate throughout her early childhood, there was still the continuous pressure from the inner nature which said: 'A foot is not this shape.'

That spiritual pressure is for us continuous. It goes on all the time.

Many people have found their time here at Keswick to be the occasion of spiritual crisis. Looking back I would say the same. I came here around forty-five years ago for the first time. There was a crisis in my life then. Many of us experience crises of different kinds, from time to time, at different stages, through our Christian lives. But the fact remains that sanctification is not a crisis but a process. If you are a new or new-ish Christian, then before you there lies a long, varied process, a demanding and exhilarating process of spiritual development. Every day will bring some new thing for you to grasp with both hands, to say 'no' to that and 'yes' to this. If you are an old or old-ish Christian—well, the process still hasn't stopped. There are still new stages as we press on through life, which God the Holy Spirit has designed for you. We're here today again to say 'no' to this and 'yes' to that—to stop being conformed to this world, and to go on being transformed by the renewing power of His Spirit in your mind.

There are parts of F. W. H. Myers' poem 'St Paul' which have stuck in my mind since I first read it many years ago, including these lines:

> Let no man think that sudden, in a minute,
> all is accomplished and the work is done;
> though with Thine earliest dawn Thou shouldst begin it,
> scarce were it ended in the setting sun.

That amazing process will be going on throughout our lives as we say, 'Lord, on the basis of the theology that You've shown me, that grand theme of salvation which focuses on the cross of Christ and the mercy of God; and in view of the worship that I give You in return for it, which is the service of my whole life, every moment and every day; I want that sanctifying process to go on through the whole of the life You give me here below.'

That is the essence of this demanding, exhilarating life of the practice of holiness.

2 : The Law We Are to Obey
Romans 13:1–14

The concern of the Keswick Convention now, as always, is that God's Spirit, speaking in and through God's word, should touch and change lives and send changed people back into the world. The object of the exercise is the same as the title I have chosen for these Bible Readings: 'the practice of holiness', which is practical holy living.

There's an old-fashioned word for that: 'piety'. As the apostle Paul moves on from the first tremendous eleven chapters of Romans (his basic comprehensive theology) into chapter 12, he is saying, 'Now this is piety! This is the way true Christian theology is to be lived out.' Used correctly, this word describes a person who is doing his best to live out, in terms of Romans 12 and onwards, the great truths of Romans 1–11.

There are several related words related to 'piety'. *Pietism* was a spiritual movement that began in the seventeenth century on the continent of Europe; its members have an honourable record of testimony to some of the great truths of the Christian faith. *Pietistic* is quite a different matter. It is a word with bad connotations. It means getting into a little holy huddle of inward-looking Christians who are concerned simply with boosting each other's spiritual feelings and are not greatly concerned with the world outside.

The Amish people in Pennsylvania and other parts of the north-eastern United States are likewise an admiral group of Christian people. Though they originate in Europe, they have different roots to those of Pietism. But the popular perception of people like the Amish community is that they are pietistic, that they withdraw from the world, wear strange old-fashioned clothes and have as little as possible to do with this modern age. A recent film depicted such a community. One of its spokesmen said to an outsider, 'We're sorry about what is happening in your world, but it has nothing to do with us.' That is a caricature of those within those communities who really love the Lord and try to serve Him. But nevertheless it is true of too many Christian people.

Keswick is not pietistic! If our message to the local community was, 'We are sorry about what is happening in your world, but it has nothing to do with us,' not only would it be a very wrong thing to say, it would also be entirely untrue. Those of us at the Keswick Convention who are seeking to grow more like Christ recognise we cannot withdraw ourselves from the world we live in. We dare not say, 'We have our Convention meetings. We're quite happy singing, praying and listening to the Bible together. What goes on out there has nothing to do with us.'

Next Saturday most of us will leave Keswick. We will go back into the world, where things go on that have a great deal to do with us. They're not church things, not 'Christian' things. They are things to do with money and mortgages and education; things of the secular world outside. And they have a great deal to do with us Christian people.

And I would say that Paul's movement from chapters 1–11, into chapter 12 and on into chapter 13 is of the very essence of the message of Keswick. He is saying, 'Here you are confronted with the truth of God; it's intended to have an effect on the way you live, in particular as you go back into the world. You are meant to represent the Lord Jesus Christ and His people in the midst of a crooked and perverse generation, among whom you are intended to shine as lights in the world' (cf Phil. 2:15).

You may have spotted that this has been hinted at in some verses in chapter 12 that we didn't look closely at yesterday. For example, verse 12, 'Be. . . patient in affliction'; verse 14, 'Bless those who persecute you'; verse 17ff, ' Do not repay anyone evil for evil. Be careful to do what is right in the eyes of everybody.

If it is possible, as far as it depends on you, live at peace with everyone. Do not take revenge, my friends.'

You could say that you experience all those things in your local church. But I think it's much more likely that Paul is speaking about the secular world, and about Christians who go out into that world and find it tough. So already you have hints in chapter 12 about the basic application of the gospel to Christian living, for people living in the real secular world.

But in chapter 13, Paul confronts this directly. And though I'm not entirely sold on three-point sermons, I have to say that just like yesterday I have three points today. For good measure (this is a real Keswick convention!) they all start with the same letter. I hope you'll find that these three Ls arise naturally from the text of Romans 13.

First, in verses 1–7, the law, which has governed the life of the people of God for the whole time that God has regarded them as His holy nation; around 3,500 years. They have lived under what you might call national laws ever since God constituted them in the time of Moses at Mount Sinai. From then until now, God has given them a law to govern their lives, not only in Old Testament days but in New Testament days as well.

In verses 8–10, we shall find Paul speaking about the love which has been the mainspring of that law, about the way God's people are expected to live and the rules they are expected to follow. The mainspring of that framework has been love, again from the very beginning (it is back there at Sinai), remains so right through until the present day, and will be to the end.

And in verses 11–14, we shall see Paul speaking about the light which shines back upon the life of the people of God, from the end, covering the whole of that long period when God's people seek to live according to His law.

You can add a fourth L: the life of God's people, with its law and its love and its light.

Law (12:1–7)

Paul is not speaking about a framework of religious, Christian or spiritual law, but the framework of law in which all of us live as

members of human society. There is something very like it back
in the Gospels. We shall find this with each of these sections of
Romans 13 (sections which I think Paul consciously created);
they are echoed in the words of the Lord Jesus Christ Himself,
in the same order. Look for example back at Mark 12:13–17 and
the story about taxes to Caesar and who owes what to whom.
Jesus says that very pregnant and mind-stretching thing, that we
are to 'give to Caesar what is Caesar's and to God what is God's'
(Mark 12:17). The truth that is concentrated in those words is
opened out for us here in Romans 13:1–7. It is a truth which I
think can surprise even instructed Christians today, and, even if
it doesn't surprise us, will certainly stretch us. Nevertheless, as
I was saying yesterday, it is rooted in the theological soil of
Romans 1–11.

The law means two things. It is firstly,

*The law is an obligation on the people of God both before and
after conversion*
It's certainly there before we are converted. Paul has already said
a great deal on this matter in Romans. Look at the opening
verses of chapter 8: 'Therefore, there is now no condemnation
for those who are in Christ Jesus, because through Christ Jesus
the law of the Spirit of life set me free from the law of sin and
death' (Rom. 8:1–2) You could say that the wonderful things in
that remarkable chapter all have to do with our freedom from the
old, unconverted life and everything that goes along with it.
From all of that, from all its implications and all its consequences, we have been set free from the law of sin and death.

Go back a chapter and you will find Paul making it plain that
among other things, this freedom is a freedom from law. In
Romans 7:4, he speaks about having 'died to the law'; in 7:6,
about having 'been released from the law'. The law is a bad thing.
We know that it's a good thing—Paul says so elsewhere—but it's
a bad thing in that it's painful, irksome and fearsome. We listen
to God's law and it frightens us. What a wonderful thing it is to
be freed from that law and to leave it behind us!

In another letter, Paul speaks of the law in a verse many of us
know from the Authorised Version: 'The law was our school-

master to bring us unto Christ, that we might be justified by faith' (Gal. 3:24, AV). The law had a big stick, and that was intended to bring us to Christ. Bunyan's Pilgrim is sent by Mr Worldly-Wiseman to be told by Mr Legality what to do to be free of his burden. But he finds the route overhung by a great high looming hill from which flames shoot and a strange voice utters dreadful things. That's the law. 'The commandment came, sin sprang to life and I died' (Rom. 7:9). When I realised what God was telling me to do, all that nonsense about 'Just show me what to do and I'll do it and I'll be all right,' simply evaporated. I realised I could never do it. The law frightens me. What a relief it will be one day to be free from it!

And it is from the law that eventually the pilgrim finds his way to the narrow gate, and to the hill where the cross stands. And there, because of something that someone else did for him, the burden of all that he has done wrong falls off his back. That's a great truth. It is at conversion that the dreadful things that the law is saying to the unconverted man are finally silenced.

A century later Augustus Toplady wrote that tremendous hymn: 'A debtor to mercy alone, of covenant mercy I sing.' If I were presenting all the law-keeping that I've done to God, He would count it as nothing and less than nothing. All I need is mercy. 'And I found it,' says Toplady. 'And now. . .'

> The terrors of law and of God
> With me can have nothing to do;
> My Saviour's obedience and blood
> Hide all my transgressions from view.

Toplady's hymn is very Romans. He's got the nub of the matter. He rejoices that what God's law said to him before he was converted has now been silenced, because Jesus has both obeyed that law in Himself, and obtained forgiveness for all that multitude of occasions when the sinner broke that law.

So we are free from the law. We've left it all behind us. It was an obligation before we were converted; now we have nothing to do with it and it has nothing to do with us—except that we then discover, once we are converted, that lo and behold, the law arises again! It's the same law, but somehow it looks different. We are looking at the same thing, but now it's bathed in the light of the cross. It is as if a gate opens up before us, and God says, 'This is the way you are to go. The same old law which you so feared in the days before you came to the cross is now your guide. It was never the way *to* life, but now that you've found life by faith this is the way *of* life.' Good works, which God has prepared for us to walk in (cf Eph. 2:10)—the law of God is still there. It is not the cause, but the consequence of salvation, that God's people do their best to obey God's law.

It was there in the very beginning in this order. For all that the New Testament tells us about the terrors of the law of God, we need to remember that way back when the law was first given in the time of the Exodus, the law was given to people who had already been redeemed. It was the mercy and grace of God which met them first and brought them out of Egypt, which laid the foundations for a law which was then meant to be their delight. It is only those who somehow missed out on the experience of the Exodus and never actually grasped for themselves what redemption meant who found the law such a dreadful thing. But for all God's people down the ages, who have begun with redemption, the law has been found to be a delight. Starting with Moses bringing God's people out into a new life, you go on to the kind of things that the Psalms say so often: God's law is something that thrills me. I love it. It's no longer a restriction and a painful, irksome, fearful thing.

Paul speaks about that in Romans 6. Didn't I tell you it was all growing there in the soil of the theology of Romans 1–11? Once 'you were slaves to sin, you were free from the control of righteousness' (6:20). Then God redeemed you and set you free; you began a new life and you found yourself in verse 22: 'you have been set free from sin and have become slaves to God'— you are back with the law again, but in an entirely different sense. You are a slave to the righteousness of God. You go His way because you want to, and He sets before you the same old law which has now become your delight.

It's from all that theological truth that we move on into chapter 12 and the chapters that follow. All the rules in chapters

12, 13 and onwards are the application of God's law, post-conversion.

But chapter 13 takes us on one step further.

The law is an obligation both inside and outside the Christian community

Just as the law was left behind when we came to Christ but reappears now that we are in Christ, so the law applies inside the Christian fellowship, and yet when we go out into the world we find that there is still law there. Verses 1–7 raise problems for Christian faith. It is a very necessary but difficult passage, and some have made very heavy weather of it. What Paul appears to be saying about the Christian's relation to the secular state can be very hard to grasp.

Verse 1, 'Every one must submit himself to the governing authorities, for there is no authority except that which God has established. The authorities that exist have been established by God.'—'What?' you retort. 'When I think of some of the authorities that have held sway in this world of ours. . .' Can Alexander the Great, Julius Caesar, Atilla the Hun, and Napoleon, who used their secular authority for personal aggrandisement and to ride over the bodies of other people in pursuit of their wishes—can those four terrible historical figures really have been established by God? Is it really true that there is no authority except that which God has established? Did God set up Nazi Germany, Stalin's Russia, Amin's Uganda and Pol Pot's Cambodia? And verse 2: do we really have to obey the kind of ruler who sets up such regimes with all their wicked laws? Verse 3: 'Rulers hold no terror for those who do right, but for those who do wrong'—Oh, come on! Can you really say that that is true of the sort of regimes I've just mentioned? Conversely, verse 4, 'He is God's servant to do you good. But if you do wrong, be afraid, for he does not bear the sword for nothing.' Yet it's the other way round under so many of these governments and dictators and tyrants. What is Paul talking about?

Look at verse 5: what if they tell me to do something which in conscience I can't do? Commentators tell us that verse 5 is actually the clue; it is not only the reason why we should normally obey the laws of governments, it is also the limit of our obedience to them. There may well come a time when conscience itself says, 'This is wrong. Don't do it, even if it means civil disobedience.'

We've not yet come to that pass in Britain. What should we do if it did? I think Romans 13 would say, conscience rules over all. You will find this demonstrated frequently in the book of Daniel, particularly in chapters 3 and 6, where God-fearing people are deeply immersed in a secular culture. There comes a point when Daniel's three friends say, 'We will not do that,' and they are prepared to be thrown into the fiery furnace for conscience's sake. Daniel says, 'I will not stop praying, even if the king does make a foolish law forbidding prayer.' And he is thrown into the den of lions, for conscience's sake.

Isn't that the spirit we see in the book of Acts when the apostles are arraigned before the authorities—they were religious authorities who should have known better—and told not to proclaim the gospel? They reply, 'Is it better to obey you, or to obey God? You know the answer. We obey God, for conscience's sake.'

Paul is not talking about the hard cases. He is not talking about difficult governments. He knows that he himself lives under a secular government that is going to cause him great difficulties and bring great suffering to the Christian church. But what he is talking about is the *principle* of government. He is talking about the structure of all human society. He is saying, I believe, that framework is better than anarchy; it is God's gift, and not only to His own people, that He should lay down rules within He expects human beings to live. It is His gift, to all those millions of people who don't recognise Him and care nothing for Him, that there should be a framework of law instead of a society which has fallen into anarchy. That is God's mercy to pagan society as well as to the God-fearing church. What He says about Himself in respect to the church, in 1 Corinthians 14:35, 'God is not a God of disorder but of peace', must be true about the world as well.

It's very interesting that out of the enormous number and variety of laws he could have used, Paul chooses to take as an example the law of taxation (verses 6 and 7). Why? Verse 6: 'This is also why you pay taxes, for the authorities are God's servants, who give their full time to governing.' It's the principle of the stipend, which is the way that ministers of religion are usually paid. A stipend is not like a salary, which is money paid in respect of work done. It is the other way round. It is a payment to you of enough money to live on, so that you are freed to do your work. In verse 6 Paul seems to be saying that civil servants are really paid stipends in order for them to live, because they are devoting their full time to government.

What a curious thing. Would you ever have thought of bracketing the ordained ministry with the Inland Revenue? R. C. Sproul points out that the Old Testament Levites are the only people in the Old Testament who are to be supported by the gifts of God's people (cf Num. 18). It's the only place in the Old Testament where God's people are told to provide cash for somebody else's living. The only other place in Scripture is here, in the New Testament, where we are expected to pay our gifts to the tax authorities to enable them to get on with the full-time work of running the country. Isn't that extraordinary?

I wonder whether Paul selected that particular type of law because he is saying, 'It is vitally important in the way God intends to run, not just the church but the world, that there should be a framework. And civil frameworks have to be paid for. So it is proper for Christian people, along with everybody else, to contribute the means by which governments can give us an order within which to live.' I find that a remarkable insight; a law which applies not only within the Christian community but outside it as well. The whole of society, the church and the world, is meant to operate within God's framework of law.

And everywhere, we find that framework. From the Exodus onwards, God gives first of all His own holy nation a framework of law in which to live, then later he gives to all the other nations, the gentiles outside, that inestimable privilege by a God whom they do not recognise. In Romans 13:1–7, God says, 'I want you, sinners though you are, although you rebel against Me, to be able to live a decent life within a framework of law.'

Love (13:8–10)

Some commentators suggest that these chapters are a patchwork of subjects stitched together in no particular order. In verses 1–7 it suddenly came into the apostle's mind to say something about the law and the State and such matters, and he thought it would fit there. Just before that he had been talking about love, as the NIV captions 12:9–21. Now, having made his detour to talk about submission to the authorities, he suddenly decides in 13:8 that he has something more to say about love.

Such randomness seems to me to be totally alien to Paul's mind. You would be more likely to find it in James, whose mind does tend to work like that, but not in Paul. I detect connections everywhere else in Paul's teaching, an integration of what he is teaching. And I believe that in verses 8–10 he is moving on to a subject closely related to what has gone before.

It's still all about law. 'There is an intimate connection between what I've been saying about the Christian's life in secular society and what I'm going to say now about love; because love has been the mainspring of law ever since the beginning. Law is the machinery, love is what makes it work.'

In a very helpful commentary on Romans, *The Gospel as it Really Is* (1979), Stuart Olyott pictures the relationship between law (13:1–7) and love (13:8–10) as being like an explosive charge and a gun barrel. He says, 'Love propels the bullet and God's Law directs it. Neither is any good on its own' (p. 128). You must have both, he says: the law says 'This is the way to fire,' and then love provides the power. That is why, I think, Paul goes on to speak about love in these three verses. He's very much aware of what he is saying here.

Paul draws on his own knowledge of Scripture

He's already in this letter spoken about obedience to the law; we have to obey what the authorities tell us to do as long as it's within our conscience. And he's spoken about obedience to the law as a duty, indeed as a debt—it is something that we ought to do, which we owe to the governing authorities to do. We are to love in a similar way: 'Let no debt remain outstanding except the continuing debt to love one another.' Already in his own writings, in what we call the Scriptures, Paul is making that link between law and love.

But it also springs from our Lord's teaching. I linked the first paragraph to Jesus' words in Mark 12. Go further on in Mark 12 and you will find that this is Jesus' next theme too. He moves from obeying the government (giving taxes to Caesar), to loving. 'Of all the commandments, which is the most important?' the lawyer asked Jesus (Mark 12:28). ' "The most important one," answered Jesus, "is this. . . 'Love the Lord your God with all your heart and with all your soul and with all your mind and with all your strength.' The second is this: 'Love your neighbour as yourself.' There is no commandment greater than these."

The law says that love is the great commandment. Not only Paul, but Jesus Himself said it. Why? Well, what we find in the Gospel is Jesus Himself referring back to still earlier Scripture, such as Leviticus 19:18 and many others.

It's built in from the beginning, you see. 'In those bad old days'—as some uninstructed Christians perceive them to be—'when God's people laboured under the burden of the law—' What nonsense! In the days of the law, the law itself was saying, 'The heart of me is that you love; you love God and you love your neighbour.'

It's all there in Scripture.

Paul draws on his own apostolic perception
The Holy Spirit of God has shown him, as the apostle of Jesus Christ, the overall perspective—the kind of thing we've seen in that tremendous theology of chapters 1–11.

Tucked away in Leviticus 19 is the half-verse 18b: 'Love your neighbour as yourself.' Preaching on this some years ago I decided to have most of Leviticus 19 read out beforehand, and the congregation found themselves listening to prohibitions against such things as planting fields with two kinds of seed, wearing clothes woven of two types of material, and clipping the edges of one's beard. How strange that this amazing verse 18b is buried among such a crowd of other things! But stand back a little bit, and by the time you get to Mark 12 you can look back and realise that Leviticus 19:18b dominates the verses around it. And by the time you get to Romans 13, written from the perspective of Paul the apostle, you discover that Leviticus 19:18b is the fulfilment of all the laws. It is the outstanding commandment.

Paul draws on his own Jewish background

Most of us have grown up in a Western secular society, and the pressure of the world around us, spoken of at the beginning of chapter 12, has caused some of us think more than we should—and in an unbiblical way—about love. So many today think that the most intense kind of love is falling in love, or even infatuation; that as love goes on, it becomes less intense. A long-term commitment isn't quite love as that first fine careless rapture was, not in the same way. Beyond that is family love, and beyond that, love for your children; then the love you have for your friends in church, and the love for the great world outside—it's all love, but it becomes more and more diluted. That's how many modern people regard love.

How alien that idea was to the people of God in Old Testament days! They understood love as something permeating every relationship in society. All Abraham's children who knew what redemption was and who were living the life of faith, who had begun with the Exodus, knew that as they moved on into life under the glorious delights and law of God, all the way through in every relationship there was the same love that would make it all work.

That's partly why I believe verses 8–10 are not separate. Romans 13 is not a miscellany of bits and pieces. It grows directly out of what Paul has been saying about the Christian's life in secular society. 'Because you are to love people, I want you to live as a good citizen in the world.'

Let me give you one tiny practical example, from a little book called *The Last Word on Guidance* by Phillip Jensen and Tony Payne (1991). 'God's plan to make us like Christ is more detailed and intricate than most of us have ever imagined,' say the authors, and go on to discuss what the Bible might have to say about how to drive a car. They demonstrate that it has a great deal to say; that loving our neighbour as ourselves has considerable implications for our behaviour on the road, that biblical comments on how we should treat our enemies have much to tell us about our attitude to inconsiderate fellow-motorists, and so on. 'God has lots of detailed guidance about driving, and it all hinges on love.'

You could multiply that kind of example endlessly. The distinctive Christian witness in the world confronts all the selfishness that we see around us with Christian care and consideration.

Light (13:11–14)

This last paragraph again is not an example of Paul's mind leaping like a grasshopper on to something new. His is an integrated mind, which follows on from what he has just been saying. 'You are to do this,' he says, 'the kind of thing I've just been speaking about. You are to practise the Christian life in society under the law of God, in the light that shines back upon your way of life, from the day of the end.'

The future

In verse 11 he speaks about 'our salvation' when the Lord Jesus returns, history comes to an end and we finally see our salvation come to its fullness in heaven. 'It's almost here,' he says, 'the day has practically arrived.'

Commentators devote much time to the question of whether Paul and the early church really believed that the return of Christ was to happen in their lifetime—which of course, it didn't. Were they disappointed? Well, the fact of the matter is that Paul and others in the New Testament say that the day of the Lord—the coming of our salvation, the end of time—is near and at hand, in two different senses.

If you travel by train from Bristol to Gloucester, you will see that near Stonehouse in Gloucestershire the main London to Gloucester line approaches yours. The two sets of tracks get closer and closer until they are running side by side: four parallel railway tracks. They don't actually connect for another mile,

near Standish. Now, in what sense is the meeting of those two
railway lines 'near'? It depends what you mean.

Verse 11, 'Our salvation is nearer now than when we first
believed.' That is Standish Junction, where your train will
suddenly clatter over a set of points and the one line will actually
connect with the other. That moment is drawing nearer and
nearer, moment by moment as you travel. But in a different
sense, ever since the line approached from Stonehouse it has
been equally near. That is what Paul is talking about in verse 12.
The day is almost here, it is always imminent, it is right there,
you have only to look out of the window to see that the day is at
hand. The Lord is at hand, the time is at hand. Philippians,
Revelation, the first and last chapters of Revelation all use this
same phrase. It is right here, and we are to live (and here's our
word) in the light of it.

At the hotel where the Convention speakers and counsellors
are staying, Helen Cook pointed out to us at prayers this
morning that every good gardener is concerned for the future; it
is of the essence of gardening. She cited one great gardener as
always having in mind 'the visual image of the beauty that is yet
to be.'

It's in that sense that we live our lives in the light of His
coming. Everything is seen, so to speak, with an eye to the
future. Paul is saying, 'Have a visual image of the beauty that is
yet to be, and let your life here be framed, shaped and coloured
by what you see coming.' In one sense it is right here even now;
in another sense it is drawing nearer and nearer, moment by
moment.

The present

But Paul is also looking to the present. The end is near in that
other sense. So, he says, 'Let's have some action' (verses 12 ff).
He urges the putting off and the putting on which is the practice
of holiness, practical holy living; putting off the deeds of dark-
ness and putting on the armour of light—the things which
belong to that coming day, to that adjacent world which is right
here and yet coming nearer. And just as there was significance in
Paul's choice of one particular branch of law in verses 6 and 7, so

there is I think a particular reason why he chooses to identify one particular kind of sin in verse 13.

Why does he choose to mention 'orgies and drunkenness. . . sexual immorality and debauchery. . . dissension and jealousy'? Because they are the sins of the night, they are the sins of dark places, they are the sins of privacy, and of the secret place, the 'in' group and the personal relationship. They are not part of 'the armour of light', but sins that are undisciplined and lax and therefore opposed to law. Whatever is self-indulgent and lustful is opposed to love. Paul is saying, 'Don't do these things, especially the kind of things I list in verse 13. They don't belong with light, and law, and love. Put them aside, and instead put on the armour of light, as you go out into the world.' He's still talking about the world, he's still talking about the law which governs us as we go out to represent God in the world outside.

I cannot leave Romans 13 without quoting from Augustine, that great saint who sixteen centuries ago was converted to Christ. You may read the account of his conversion in his *Confessions*. He had been a wild young man kicking over the traces in all directions, and from experience he knew exactly those things which Paul says are not appropriate for those who want to live for God within the framework of God's law. His life was filled with such things. But he was dissatisfied with his life. One day he was staying in a friend's house in Milan, and he was sitting in the garden.

> I was saying this sort of thing and weeping in the most bitter contrition of my heart. And I heard a voice as if it were a boy or girl in a neighbouring house, singing over and over again, 'Take and read, take and read.' And I began to wonder whether it was usual for children in some kind of game to sing such words, I couldn't remember if I'd heard anything like it. So I got up interpreting it to be none other than a command from heaven, and I opened the book I'd been reading and read the first chapter that my eyes lighted upon. And this was the passage upon which my eyes first fell: 'Not in orgies and drunkenness, not in promiscuity and debauchery, not in dissension and jealousy, but rather clothe yourselves with the Lord Jesus Christ and do not think

about how to gratify the desires of the sinful nature.' I read no further, I didn't need to, for instantly, as the sentence ended, it was as if my heart was flooded with the light of peace and all the shadows of doubt melted away.

I quote the great Augustine in particular because he was one of the most influential men in Christian history, not only in the church but in the world. It's said that his writings massively influenced almost every sphere of Western thought in the centuries that followed. He was a man who, both within the community of God's people and when he went out into secular society, was concerned that the law of God should rule and men should know what it was to live within that framework.

And God can do that for us too.

3: The Liberty We Are to Enjoy
Romans 14:1–15:13

We've already heard quite a lot about freedom in Romans 12 and
13. On Monday morning we thought about the life that we are to
live when Christ has set us free from the old life of sin. Yesterday
we thought about the law we are to obey when the law of the
Spirit of life has set us free from the law of sin and death. Now
today we come the liberty we are to enjoy—freedom itself. And
we shall find that this kind of liberty is as paradoxical and as
mind-stretching as anything that we have found in Romans so
far.

Introduction

I am going to make four introductory points relatively briefly,
and then divide our long passage into four sections. As introduction, I want to touch on the background of this chapter-and-a-
half, the division that it describes, the counterpart in our modern
world to what we find there in that ancient world, and then the
problem which is a part of it.

The background

In New Testament times some churches were almost made up of
Jewish Christians, such as the church in Jerusalem right at the
outset. Others were largely Gentile, like the church in Antioch.
But most churches were somewhere within that spectrum, and
were mixtures of Jews and Gentiles. And the contact between

the Jewish community and the Gentile community within a particular church was not always easy.

There were problems in the Antioch church, which was largely Gentile, when people from Jerusalem came to visit; you can read about it in Galatians 2. There were great debates in the church in Jerusalem when people came from Antioch with news of what was going on there, and you can find that in Acts 15. There was a convergence, I won't say conflict (though sometimes it was) between the two different cultures within one particular church. The Roman church, to which Paul wrote this letter, is a classic example. There were Jews and Gentile Christians within it. Our passage today gives us one example of the kind of difficulties that this caused.

The division
The division spoken of here is not actually labelled as between Jews and Gentiles but as between the strong and the weak. That comes many times, as you will have seen.

There are various interpretations of what Paul had in mind when he spoke of the strong people and the weak people in the church in Rome. But I think that verses 2 and 5 of chapter 14 are useful clues. Verse 2: 'One man's faith allows him to eat everything, but another man, whose faith is weak, eats only vegetables.' There could be many reasons for making that sort of distinction. But when you add verse 5, and you find that 'one man considers one day more sacred than another; another man considers every day alike,' it is perhaps a pointer to church divisions arising from cultural background; whether you had a Jewish background or a Gentile background. The issue of food laws and the observance of days might very well be the people with Jewish backgrounds saying, 'There are certain rules in the Old Testament about what you can eat' (today they are called kosher rules), 'and there are certain holy days in the Jewish calendar which we really ought to observe. If we are going to be God-fearing Jews, even if we've now been converted, these things are still important.'

I think it's highly likely that the division between strong and the weak had something to do with what your background was.

By and large, though there's obviously considerable overlap, it would be people from a Gentile background who said, 'What do all those Jewish laws matter? We are free from that sort of thing.' And Christians from a Jewish background would say, 'Of course they matter! They are part of God's revelation in the Scriptures, and we ought to observe them.' So there the Gentiles would have been the strong ones and the Jews the weak ones, as I shall explain later.

The strong people were saying that all those Old Testament duties and obligations were shackles from which Christians have now been liberated. The weak were saying, 'Well, of course Christ has set us free from feeling we have to earn our salvation by obeying the law. But surely there are still things that we ought to do; God still has expectations of us, which He's set out in Scripture.'

This is not so fundamentally dangerous serious a division as that which led to the confrontation between Peter and Paul in the church in Antioch, where Paul realised that the distinction between the two groups there was actually eroding the foundations of the gospel itself. This division concerns what are called in 14:1 'disputable matters'. The sixteenth-century reformers called such matters the *adiaphora*—'things that don't matter very much'. For these Christians, who had been truly liberated, the division was between those who thought they had been liberated a lot and those who thought they'd been liberated, but not quite so much.

The counterpart

What is the modern counterpart to the division in that New Testament church? John Stott, in his commentary on Romans, writes:

> If we presume it was in those days a matter of people's attitudes to Old Testament rules and regulations, what are the equivalents in the modern church of 'disputable matters'? Matters on which it was not necessary for all Christians to agree; adiaphora, or matters of indifference, whether, as here, they were customs and ceremonies, or whether they were secondary beliefs which are

not part of the gospel or the creed, matters on which Scripture does not clearly pronounce.

In our day we might mention such matters as the mode of baptism—immersion, or sprinkling? Episcopal confirmation —is it a legitimate part of Christian initiation? The exchanging of wedding rings—hotly contested by seventeenth-century Puritans; the use of cosmetics, or jewellery, or alcohol; and such matters as which charismatic gifts are available and/or important, whether miraculous signs and wonders are intended to be frequent or infrequent, how Old Testament prophecy has been or will be fulfilled, when and how the millennium will be established, the relation of history to eschatology and the precise nature of both heaven and hell.

There's a packet! I dare say we could add even more. But how can we tell exactly which really are the matters which are indifferent?

The problem

Christians will differ over what is disputable and what is indisputable. Everyone says, 'Well I believe this very strongly, you can take it or leave it,' because none of us will actually admit to being among the weak. We all think that we are part of the strong faction in the church in Rome; 'the weak' is the other lot, they're the ones with the problem. Everyone says, 'I believe strongly I have been freed from the old life, I've been freed from the law of sin and death.'

Paul, more than most of us, would say, 'We've been freed from this, and freed from that'; but he would draw the line at saying we're free from the Ten Commandments, surely. You've got to draw the line somewhere, and beyond that line things are important and necessary. So—where do you draw the line?

'I've been freed from all sorts of dreadful things in my past sinful life. I've been freed from all kinds of things that other Christians are bruised by. But I draw the line at pre-tribulationist dispensationalism; and I have to draw the line at infant baptism, *that's* not disputable. I have to draw the line at the Toronto Blessing. I have to draw the line at the ordination of women.' Do you see what I'm saying? What becomes a test of orthodoxy? We are free in all sorts of areas, but at some particular point I find a test of orthodoxy. I draw a line and I say, beyond this point, if you don't believe what I believe, you must be wrong. This is not disputable.

Then somebody else says, 'But this is very disputable.' And that's the problem.

It's not the thing in itself. It is none of these things in themselves. In Romans 14 and 15 Paul is not arguing the toss about any particular matter. He is talking about how you cope with the basic problem of where to draw the line between what is and is not disputable or indisputable.

Now, Paul himself is an apostle of Jesus Christ; when he says what he believes, he is drawing the line in the right place. And we have to come clean at the outset and concede that Paul explicitly sides with the strong party in Rome. He says as much in 14:14. 'As one who is in the Lord Jesus'—this is an unusually strong statement for Paul—'I am fully convinced that no food'—'nothing', more correctly—'is unclean in itself.' He even attaches the label to himself: 'We who are strong' (15:1). 'I side with you people who reckon you are strong, and not with the weak; I think they are wrong,' says Paul.

Nevertheless these chapters are not concerned with Paul lecturing and brow-beating the weak and saying how immature they are, and what a feeble grasp they have of Bible truth because they believe as they do. He recognises that the real problem is disagreement over where to draw the line. What he really wants to get across is that though he sides with the strong, he is prepared to accept those who think differently on this type of question. Both weak and strong, he says, ought to do that. And here he sets forth how it is, in practice, that Christians are to find liberty in their relationships, even with those from whom they differ on matters such as those I've mentioned.

Finding freedom in servanthood (14:1–12)

We find as elsewhere that what Paul says here has its roots in the Gospels, in the words of Jesus Himself. For example John 8:36,

' So if the Son sets you free, you will be free indeed.' The apostle
Paul opens out that great statement as to what it means to find
freedom in Christ. Verse 3 tells us something that can happen in
a church like the one in Rome, or like yours, or like mine. One
person has certain convictions about the practice of holiness. He
believes that it's all right to eat anything. He tends to despise
those who have scruples about such matters. Conversely, the
person who has scruples and has problems with rules and
regulations tends to condemn the person who feels he has the
freedom. So the strong despises the weak and the weak despises
the strong.

What ought to happen is that instead of regarding each other
in this very negative way, all alike should be looking instead to
their common master. It comes out so clearly. Verse 4: 'Who are
you to judge someone else's servant? To his own master he stands
or falls.' Verse 6: 'He who regards one day as special [the weak
Jewish brother], does so to the Lord. He who eats meat [the
strong Gentile brother], eats to the Lord, for he gives thanks to
God; and he who abstains, does so to the Lord and gives thanks
to God.' Verse 10: 'We will all stand [all of us alike] before God's
judgement seat.' What matters is not how we judge one another,
but how God judges each of us. And it is to him that we are to
look.

As a good Jew, Paul must have known the Psalter by heart. Did
he have in mind those lovely words, 'As the eyes of slaves look to
the hand of their master, as the eyes of a maid look to the hand
of her mistress, so our eyes look to the LORD our God' (Psa.
123:2)? We will be a great deal less concerned about despising or
condemning what our fellow Christian is doing, if our eyes are
on our Master to see what He thinks about things. And if every
Christian is eager to serve God and to obey what God clearly
says to him or to her, the problem begins to evaporate.

Let me try to spell out to you once more what the problem is.
The weak party are those drawing the line sooner. 'Up to this
point,' they say, 'we have been free from all the rules and the
laws. But beyond it, there are quite a lot of things that we ought
to do, and we regard people who play fast and loose with those
considerations as very worldly people.' The strong draw the line

much later, and go much further: 'We are free; we are free here. . . we are free there. . . we are free in all sorts of areas. Certainly there is a line. Beyond it, there are things that we ought to do. But to make such a song and dance about all these very obvious and simple things as the weak are doing—well, if they think we are worldly, we think they are silly.'

That ought not to happen. And so the apostle says, 'No! That is all too likely to happen in any Christian fellowship, but grace and charity and spiritual perception ought to be opening your eyes to see that I am truly, honestly seeking only to serve the Lord. And I ought to have my eyes opened to see that you are truly, honestly, seeking only to serve the Lord, even if we differ as to how to do it. But if I can see that you truly have been set free from the law as a way to life; that you believe as I believe that we are saved by grace and not by anything we do; that you've taken upon yourself the yoke of the law which is now the law of love, not as the way to life which it can never be, but as *the* way of life—then I see in you a Christian brother and a sister, however much we differ; not only on disputable things but as to what those disputable things are. If I see you as being like me, a servant of the Lord whose heart-concern is simply to do what He tells us, then all these lesser problems will begin to be put in their proper place. In that common servanthood, the differences will be seen as they ought to be seen.'

One of the memorable collects of the Anglican prayer book speaks of His service as 'perfect freedom'. And as we unitedly submit to His service and see in one another the desire only to do what He wants us to do, the other things begin to take their rightful places and we begin to see what is truly important. This is the liberty that puts inessentials into their proper perspective; the liberty of servanthood.

Finding freedom in strength (14:13–23)

Paul does not actually use the word 'strong' until 15:1. But the concept of what is meant by being a strong Christian is to be found throughout our passage and especially in the latter part of chapter 14: just as the first section was about the liberty of being found as common servants of our master, so here liberty is the freedom we find in His strength.

I believe that Paul is speaking here about three kinds of strength. There is, first and most obviously,

The strength of the strong

'We who are strong' (15:1)—'I am one of you,' says Paul. 'I am a strong Christian in this respect; I believe that there are all sorts of rules which I do not need to observe because I am a Christian. I am strong, and I am chiefly addressing strong Christians.'

When in 14:1 he says, 'Accept him whose faith is weak,' he is obviously speaking to strong Christians like himself. In 14:14 he describes himself 'as one who is in the Lord Jesus' and is 'fully convinced' that there all sorts of freedoms in Christ—in particular, regarding the food laws. 'The food laws do not matter,' he says. 'Nothing is unclean in itself. That is my stance.' He draws the line a great deal further out and further on than many Christians would feel it right to do.

But what strength of character the man has! Concerning this passage F. F. Bruce writes, 'So completely emancipated was Paul from spiritual bondage that he was not even in bondage to his own emancipation.' Which, to put in briefer and simpler words, means that Paul never felt bound to be free, though he *was* free; he never felt he had to assert or parade his freedom, to ride roughshod over the feelings of other Christians who had problems about various matters. Far from feeling it necessary to say, 'You can and ought to be free like me' (which he never said), he said, 'Brother, sister, if you've got a scruple over that particular matter, I have the strength of character not to parade my freedom in something that bothers you. And if it's going to be a help to you, I will not be free in that matter when I'm in your presence. I know in my own heart,' he says, 'between myself and God, there is nothing about that particular thing that really matters. But when you are around, and I know that to you it does matter—well, bless you brother, bless you sister, I will not be an offence to you. I won't be a stumbling block to you.'

He says something similar in 1 Corinthians 10: this is a very clear and concise statement of it. He is free from so many traditions, rules and regulations and holy days which Jewish Christian brethren still felt important. He is free from the kosher laws, free from so much that he himself inherited, but he is *not* free from the obligation to limit his own freedom if that would benefit his brothers and sisters. He is not free from the obligation to refrain from insisting on his rights. That is an obligation that still remains in place for this very free Christian man. 'If it will help my brother or my sister who is bothered by something which does not bother me in the least, then I am prepared to be bothered by it too in these particular circumstances.' That is the strength of the strong. It's a great thing to covet, isn't it?

The strength of the weak

These chapters are full of paradoxes. Here's another.

Do you know these words from *Measure for Measure*, one of Shakespeare's most profound plays?

> O, it is excellent
> to have a giant's strength; but it is tyrannous
> to use it like a giant. (Act II ii)

The weak have a strength that can be tyrannous; having many scruples of their own, being very troubled about all sorts of things that many of us are not troubled about at all, it is possible for such Christians to use their problems to manipulate others and their church fellowships, using their problems as a powerful lever for getting their own way. 'We can't possibly go down this road because I am very bothered by it.' So the whole church is held up by the scruples of one Christian—scruples which do not in fact matter very much. And that is tyranny.

C. S. Lewis somewhere speaks about the distinct possibility among Christian people that a 'dog in the manger' might become a tyrant of the universe. 'I am here, and woe betide you if you try to shift me.' Everybody else has to toe the line because of the tyrannous strength of the weak brother.

But there is a third kind of strength which Paul speaks about here.

The strength of the united fellowship

He speaks of the strength of a loving and accepting fellowship where things begin to happen; where Gentile brothers and sisters and Jewish brothers and sisters, much though they may differ on secondary matters, have the strength of character to say, 'Much more important than the strong despising the weak because they are silly and the weak condemning the strong because they are worldly, is that we together "make every effort to do what leads to peace and to mutual edification." '(14:19).

I have already given you one quotation from the Book of Common Prayer. Here is something familiar to those of us who are Anglicans, from the Alternative Service Book Communion Service: 'Let us therefore pursue everything that makes for peace and builds up our common life.' That is a great strength in a united fellowship where people recognise that they do differ on a whole range of Christian matters, but that they are staying together and are prepared to shake hands on it: Jewish Christians and Gentile Christians together, the strong and the weak together; this is the liberty that accepts limitations for the sake of others. It's a great thing for us all to aim at in our own lives and fellowships.

Finding freedom in constraint (15:1–6)

Here is a freedom that is even more paradoxical. How can it be freedom when I am hemmed in, when there are bars about me? What does it mean to say you can find freedom in constraint?

Well, what is Christian freedom? Is it freedom to do what I like?

Let's take these verses through in sequence.

Verse 1: Christian freedom is not pleasing ourselves. It is a freedom constrained by obligations, a freedom in which that blessed word 'ought' reappears, The law comes back in; duties, things we have to do. What is law doing in a Christian life, a life of freedom? This is the freedom of constraint. 'We who are strong and free ought [we have the duty, we are constrained by the duty] to bear with the failings of the weak.' It may mean to put up with them, to say, 'Well, they annoy me intensely but I'm prepared to go along with them.' Or it may be the freedom to bear them, to carry them, to run our Christian lives in such a way that those who find these things to be real difficulties are somehow lifted and carried along with us, so that the difficulties become less great for them. Those of us who are strong have this obligation to bear with the failings of the weak and not to please ourselves. There is a great freedom in this sort of constraint.

Verse 2: What is the opposite of pleasing ourselves? We who are strong ought not to please ourselves, instead we are to please our neighbour. But Paul makes it very clear this doesn't mean pandering to our neighbour. It's not saying, 'If that's what you want, there, you shall have it.' That makes us highly vulnerable to manipulation, and it's not right. It is a case of pleasing our neighbour, as Paul says, 'for his good, to build him up'. That's the great constraint that is concerned with his real benefit.

Verse 3 opens this out. 'Even Christ did not please himself.' As we look at what Christ has to say here (for Paul is quoting the words of Psalm 69 as the words of Christ), we can see that what we are talking about as freedom in constraint is not simply the narrow irksomeness of our fellow Christian whom we meet Sunday by Sunday, who annoys us so intensely because he has such peculiar scruples and thinks such weird unimportant things really are important. As we consider Christ and His attitude to such things, the whole matter begins to open out. We see that freedom in constraint refers to an entire range of negative things, to all sorts of things in the Christian life that could be regarded as restraints of this kind. 'The insults of those who insult you have fallen on me.' This wonderful Psalm 69, often quoted in the New Testament as having to do with Christ and the people of Christ, is speaking here about the insults men and women offer to God. They care little about God, and God's chosen one says, 'You know, I have had the experience of all the insults with which people insult God; they actually come down on me too.'

Christ comes into the world and finds that all those unformed, unexpressed thoughts that people have, negative thoughts towards God, find expression when they see God come in the flesh. There is now somebody to level them at, and the insults of those who insulted God fall upon His chosen one. All the antagonism and opposition we find expressed for example in the opening chapter of John's Gospel—'He came into this world and He came to His own people, and His own people didn't want to know'—and all the bad things they'd ever privately, secretly, silently thought about God, they could now express to somebody. They could afford to ignore, to hate and despise and pour scorn upon a particular person, the Lord Jesus Christ. And there are great negative things, great constraints in that, when we discover that Paul is saying that the kind of insults people hurl at the unseen God, you then find they hurl at His representative here on earth.

You subsequently find it opening out still further. The same sort of negative attitudes come to the people of Christ; they find themselves in exactly the same position. They find that people don't like them either, and that all kinds of opposition, constraints and nastiness comes their way and surrounds them just as it surrounded Jesus and just as in a sense they even surround God.

And so verse 4 opens this up still further. Now Paul tells us that the whole of Scripture, everything that was written in the past, was written to teach us. The whole of Scripture is in a sense directed to the situation that we're talking about—Christian people who find themselves under constraints of this kind—it is designed to encourage us in this kind of a life. The practice of holy living will bring us into such situations, where things irk us and are problems for us, for that is what it means to try to practise a holy life in this world; a life which throughout, we will find, demands endurance and encouragement.

Now if that is so, how vital that the mutual criticism over non-essentials within a Christian fellowship which Paul is addressing in these chapters should be dealt with; that wherever you have Christians looking at other Christians and condemning them because they consider them worldly or silly, we should learn how to deal with it. It is far more important that 'in a spirit of unity' (verse 5) we learn how to confront the constraints around us, the opposition that faces the church as a whole, and all the things with which Satan wants to hem us in and confound what we are doing for the Lord. We must be united and free from this sort of to-ing and fro-ing within the fellowship.

So, 'With one heart and mouth you may glorify the God and Father of our Lord Jesus Christ' (verse 6). This is the liberty that makes a virtue of restrictions, that rejoices to find this opportunity to see what the gospel can do: it brings together Christians who differ radically from one another.

Finding freedom in unity (15:7–13)

Our last heading has been touched upon in what I've just been saying. 'Accept one another, then, just as Christ accepted you, in order to bring praise to God' (15:7). Our recognition and acceptance of each other in the Christian fellowship—however much we may differ over eschatology, baptism, the Toronto Blessing, or any such things—is intended to be modelled on Christ's acceptance of us.

One of Paul's great themes in this connection is the fact that Jesus Christ accepts Jew and Gentile alike; and that's especially appropriate if this is the division within the Roman church. The Christians in Rome find themselves divided over the matter of whether you can or can't do certain things. If that's related to whether or not you've got a Jewish background, you see, Paul is saying, 'Now Christ accepted you whether you were Jewish or Gentile. Christ has brought you together from both communities; you ought to do the same.' That's the model for our acceptance of one another.

Yet (again a great paradox) we are free to enjoy this liberty once we grasp that that sort of liberty has wholly to do with service. What did Christ come into the world as a servant to do? (verse 8). He came to bind Himself, to restrict Himself, to constrained Himself to a particular kind of servanthood, a service to both Jew and Gentile. 'I tell you that Christ has become a servant of the Jews on behalf of God's truth, to confirm the promises made to the patriarchs'—and I believe that the end of the verse should rightly be translated, 'while the Gentiles glorify God for his mercy'.

And the wonderful truth that Christ brought to the Jews as

He bound Himself to serve them was that what God had promised to their ancestors in the Jewish nation had all been fulfilled. He became a servant of the Jews for the sake of God's truth.

In what sense then did He become a servant of the Gentiles? So that they would glorify God for His mercy. They didn't have the law, they'd never obeyed it. The amazing revelation to the Gentiles was the mercy of God. He brought the truth of God for the Jews, and the mercy of God for the Gentiles. The two overlap, of course. The Jews know as much about the mercy as about the truth, the Gentiles know as much about the truth as about the mercy. But here's the thrust; Christ is prepared to come down into this world as a servant in order to bring God's people into a unity, where they are not divided by the kinds of things that divide churches like the church in Rome or, dare I say, your church or mine. He bound Himself to this tremendous project.

Verse 9 quotes Psalm 18:49, 'Therefore I will praise you among the Gentiles; I will sing hymns to your name.' What is special about that? Psalm 18 is quoted in full in 2 Samuel 22 as the words of King David. So Romans 15:9 reminds us that David says, 'Therefore I, the king of Israel, will praise you among the Gentiles.' The two are brought together.

Verse 10 quotes Deuteronomy 32:43, the words of Moses: 'Rejoice, O Gentiles, with his people.' The two are brought together.

Verse 11 quotes another psalm, Psalm 117:1, 'Praise the LORD, all you Gentiles'—'the Lord' is Yahweh, the distinctive God of Israel—hence, 'Praise the God of Israel, you Gentiles.' The two are brought together.

Finally verse 12: 'Isaiah says, "The root of Jesse" '—who stands there in the pedigree of Israel's line of kings—'will spring up, one who will arise to rule over the nations; the Gentiles will hope in him.'

Paul has drawn together four marvellous quotations from the Jewish Scriptures, every one of which speaks of the restraint which Christ put Himself under in order to bring together people who differed.

The freedom that we find in unity, the creating of a united fellowship in which all these differences, between Jew and Gentile, between the strong and the weak, over disputable things, and over which are the disputable things and where you draw the line—as John Stott says in his commentary on Galatians, on a parallel verse, 'these are differences which of course exist, but do not matter.' And that puts it in a nutshell.

In fact it is necessary that the differences should exist. It is part of God's wonderful plan that within the unity of the church we should be Jews and Gentiles together. Such differences are not to be forgotten. If anything, they are to be remembered and celebrated. Isn't it amazing that in heaven we shall all be so varied? It's the object of the exercise that we should not all become alike. There's no bland superficial unity. It is the unity of people who differ and vary from one another. So, far from finding that these differences irk us and cramp us and trouble us, far from finding them bonds and shackles, we should find that the differences between us are opportunities to rejoice in the liberty with which Christ has set us free.

Why does Paul, in the closing verses of our section here, speak three times over of hope? Verses 12–13: ' ". . . The Gentiles will hope in Him." May the God of hope fill you with all joy and peace as you trust in him, so that you may overflow with hope by the power of the Holy Spirit.' Well, the hope is the hope of heaven. It is the hope of the light of the world to come. In other words, God is opening up before us His long-term plan. He is looking towards the great consummation at the end of all things, and the return of Christ.

And he looks back even to Isaiah, who already spoke about it (verse 12); even to Moses, who'd already spoken about it (verse 10); even to David, who'd already spoken about it (verse 9). It was way back there in the very roots, the beginnings of the story of the people of God. And it looks on to the very end of the whole story that stands before us. This is God's long term plan. And it's a plan which gives us liberty, a liberty which rejoices in God's long term objectives: the liberty of unity.

4: The Leadership We Are to Follow
Romans 15:14–33

Relatively new Christians first discovering the letter to the Romans usually regard chapters 1–8 as the meat of the letter and chapters 9–16 as the 'afters'. When they get to know Romans better, they realise that from chapter 1 through to the end of chapter 11 is all great Christian teaching, whereas chapters 12–16 are the application of the doctrine. You can go further and realise that the application and the doctrine belong together, you should not separate them, so from chapter 1 to at least chapter 15:13 is an integral whole. You might then regard the passage to which we now turn as a kind of one-and-a-half chapter post-script to a fourteen-and-a-half chapters long letter.

But I think we should look at this morning's and tomorrow morning's passages like this: that certainly in a sense they are extras Paul adds to the end of his tremendous letter, but that the writer of the whole letter, postscript and all, is a man possessed by the principles of the gospel. Everything he does, says, thinks and writes is shot through with those principles. The whole machinery of his life is run on that fuel. So it's not surprising if this personal ending to the letter, on which commentators tend to spend considerably less time than on the earlier chapters, demonstrates how these principles work out in Paul's personal experience.

We can therefore see the same sort of thing at work even in the personal words with which he concludes Romans. It's interesting that the three words we used as headings in chapter 12 appear again here; it's the same gospel and the same man, even if he is writing in a different style at the end of the letter. Those three words, 'theology', 'worship' and 'sanctification', are the key to Christian living in general. That was why we used them as our headings in chapter 12. But by the same token they are also the key to God's leading in particular, in the circumstances of any particular Christian's life.

I am not going to use a three-fold structure today as I did when we were studying chapter 12. I'm going to divide what I want to say into two sections, and you'll see how our three words fit in a little later.

The way that God led Paul

'The way that God led Paul' meant an actual journey around the Mediterranean world. We have it described for us in verses 18–28. Verses 18–22 tell us that God had led His servant Paul 'from Jerusalem'. It doesn't say that was where his ministry to the Gentiles began, because it didn't. He was converted somewhere else and he began his ministry somewhere else. But it's true to say that God had led him 'from Jerusalem' in the sense that the original mission to the Gentiles, the spread of the gospel to non-Jewish people, had begun from there; and in another sense Paul's personal career before he was converted had begun in Jerusalem. Acts 22:3 tells us in his own words: 'I am a Jew, born in Tarsus of Cilicia, but brought up in this city [Jerusalem]. Under Gamaliel I was thoroughly trained in the law of our fathers and was just as zealous for God as any of you are today.' That was where his adult career had begun, even before he was converted.

The route by which God led Paul

So in two senses we could say that the missionary travels began in Jerusalem. God has led Paul from Jerusalem, 'all the way around to Illyricum'. There are maps in many Bibles showing that great arc of countries around the eastern end of the Mediterranean Sea and charting Paul's travels. In modern terms, he went from Israel, through Lebanon and Syria, into Turkey and across to Greece, up the other side of Greece to what we call Albania and on almost as far as what today we would call Croatia. And all the way, he tells us in these verses, he went as a pioneer. 'It has always been my ambition to preach the gospel where Christ was not known' (verse 20). 'I wanted to be the first person ever in those places to proclaim the gospel fully. It may have filtered through in various other ways, by individuals converted elsewhere, but I wanted this tremendous privilege of being the first, as it were, official preacher of the gospel, in all that range of lands'—that's where God has led him so far.

Verses 23–24 tell us where God seems to be leading him now. 'But now that there is no more place for me to work in these regions, and since I have been longing for many years to see you, I plan to do so when I go to Spain.' God, he believes, is leading him on to the opposite end of the Mediterranean world, right round to the far west of the Roman Empire. I suppose he would travel a great deal by land. We can imagine him taking ship to go across to Sicily, Sardinia or Corsica. He was aiming around the north-western Mediterranean Sea, I suppose up the coast of Italy, across into what is known to us as France and down the Mediterranean coast of Spain; all the way to what is now Gibraltar and what the ancients called 'the Pillars of Hercules', the mountains on either side of the Straits of Gibraltar, where you sailed out to who knew where. It was the end of the known world for most people.

'I'd like to go to the ends of the earth as a pioneer evangelist,' says the apostle Paul. 'But I would go by way of Rome. And I have to admit,' he says, 'my great ambition of always being a pioneer missionary and preaching where no one else has preached the gospel, doesn't really apply in the case of Rome.' The very fact that he is writing to a Christian church in Rome shows that he wouldn't be the first Christian to preach there. 'Nevertheless,' he says, 'I'll break my rule on this one occasion. I really would love to come to Rome, even though there I would not be received as a pioneer.'

Why? For all sorts of reasons. He wanted to see the people

there. He wanted to visit Jews and Gentile Christians in Rome. As we shall see tomorrow, Paul has many friends in Rome already. And who would not want to go to Rome? It was the centre of the world, and Paul was perfectly human.

Verses 25–28, 'But first of all God is leading me, I believe, back to Jerusalem where it all began.' It's thought that he was writing from Corinth in Greece. As he sits in the house of his friend Gaius, we can imagine him saying, 'Before I can come west to Rome and then to Spain, I have to go east just once more, back to Jerusalem. I have a collection to deliver. There have been collections in all the places I've visited, for needy people back in the mother city of Jerusalem. Christians in many places in Greece have been contributing and they've entrusted this fund to me. I want to take that back! I would like to see it received with gratitude by the Christians back in my own mother city where I was brought up and educated, where the church began and from which the gospel first spread. I must first go back to Jerusalem. Then I'll come to you, and I'll go on to Spain.'

Notice the way that God led Paul in this sense of the route in which God led Paul. Parts of it he knows well. He is absolutely sure God has led him from Jerusalem as far as Greece and right up to the borders of Illyricum. Why is he certain of that? Because it's happened. It's in the past. So you know that's what God wanted to do because He's done it.

But his desire to go to Rome and then to Spain, and his desire before that to go back to Jerusalem; in what does the leading of God consist there? The route from Corinth to Jerusalem, from Jerusalem to Rome, from Rome to Spain—in what sense is that the leading of God? How sure is Paul that that route is part of God's plan? I think we have to be candid, and say that part of it is simply what Paul would love to do. He speaks about his 'longing' to see his friends in Rome (15:23). He speaks about his ambition to always go somewhere where the gospel has not yet been preached. He speaks even of his intention: 'I *will* go to Spain and visit you one the way' (15:28). He intends to do it.

Now how much of that is he sure is the leading of God? We shall see.

The methods by which God led Paul

But first, I want to talk about the methods God used to make sure that His servant followed the His leading. How did Paul know? And it's here that I want to raise our three terms from Monday morning: 'theology', 'worship' and 'sanctification': God's method in leading Paul along that route. Remember the first of our Bible Readings. When the truth of chapters 1–11 becomes the life of chapters 12–15, that truth is the *theological* soil which the practice of holy living grows. *Worship* is the definition of what practical holy living is. And *sanctification* is the process by which practical holy living develops. It is just so here, when we look specifically at how the apostle is led by God in the service of God. Theology—'Therefore, I urge you, brothers, in view of God's mercy'; worship—'to offer your bodies as living sacrifices'; and sanctification—'Do not be conformed any longer to the pattern of this world, but go on being transformed by the renewing of your mind' (cf 12:2).

In verses 15:15–17 Paul speaks of 'the grace God gave me to be a minister of Christ Jesus to the Gentiles with the priestly duty of proclaiming the gospel of God,'—I think we can understand it better if we leave out 'proclaiming'—'so that the Gentiles might become an offering acceptable to God, sanctified by the Holy Spirit. Therefore I glory in Christ Jesus in my service to God.' It's all there in verse 16. Where is the theology? 'The gospel of God'. Where is the worship? 'I am a minister with the priestly duty of the gospel of God to make the Gentiles an offering acceptable to Him.' And where is the sanctification? The word itself is there, at least in the NIV: 'sanctified by the Holy Spirit'.

Now with those three headings in mind, by what method does God lead His servant Paul?

Theology   The first vital element is that there is a theology behind it all. That's why I disagree with the NIV's use of 'proclaiming' in verse 16. It makes it sound as if the gospel comes last in a long list, that first there was the grace God gave him (verse 15), which made him a minister with a ministry, and that ministry meant for Paul a particular duty, and that duty was proclamation, and what was to be proclaimed was—at the end of that long list—the gospel.

I believe that he is actually saying this: 'The grace God gave me to be a minister of Christ Jesus to the Gentiles, with the priestly duty of the gospel of God.' The gospel of God is priest work, to use the phrase coined by Bishop Handley Moule. All of us who are involved with the gospel are involved with priest work.

It's very important that people in any kind of Christian ministry should grasp this. I've had ordinands in my congregation who begin at the other end. They believed God gives has given the grace to do something, but they don't exactly know what. Then it begins to clarify: grace to be a minister. So you say, 'Where?' And they say, 'Oh—I suppose to the Gentiles.'

'And what sort of ministry?'

'Well, a priestly duty.'

'What does that involve?'

'Well . . . I suppose . . . ministers preach, don't they, so it's proclaiming . . .'

'And what are you going to proclaim?'

'Ah . . .' At the end of the list they begin to think about what it's all for. It's fascinating and lovely to see how this also begins to clarify, but I'm sometimes rather appalled by the folk who have a whole concept of how romantic it is to go into the ministry but have no clear idea what they are going to do when they get there. It has to be spelled out for them very carefully that's it's actually about the gospel.

It's much better to start at the other end, and say that the gospel is what surrounds us. It's all about the gospel. Your particular job in it may be to proclaim the gospel, but we all have the priestly duty which has to do with the gospel of God. The gospel is the basis of it all, the origin of the life, witness and service of every Christian, the framework within which we all operate, the theological soil (if I may return to my metaphor) in which all Christian holy living and service grows. And there has to be that basic theology, we have to know what underlies it all.

Worship   What a lot there is here about worship! 'To be a minister of Christ Jesus to the Gentiles with the priestly duty of proclaiming the gospel of God, so that the Gentiles might become an offering acceptable to God.' It's a great evangelical maxim that the word 'priest' in the usual sense has no place in Christian practice. I was ordained priest in the Church of England many years ago, but I understand that the word priest doesn't mean a priest of the Old Testament. It's a presbyter, an elder in the church of God. Priesthood is a word never used of the Christian ministry in the New Testament. It is only mentioned when the priest concerned is an Old Testament priest, or the great High Priest who is Jesus Christ. Priesthood has nothing whatever to do with a Christian ministry today, so I believe and so I hope do you.

'But,' you may object, 'what about Romans 15:16? Doesn't that undercut that great truth? Here the apostle Paul himself, no less, says that he is acting as a priest when he goes around preaching the gospel. So there *is* an Old Testament type of sacrificing priest—Paul—in the New Testament.'

But in fact it means exactly the opposite. I think what Paul is saying, when he says, 'I have a priestly ministry,' is something like this: 'Back there in those bygone days when priests offered sacrifices in a temple, that was God's system for that time only. Everything that belongs to it has been brought into our world in a different form. Where priests once offered sacrifices in temples, I am now proclaiming the gospel. That is the equivalent, and replacement, for the Old Testament priestly ministry. Do priests offer sacrifices nowadays? Well yes, in the sense that we have a gospel to proclaim. And that is what we are doing when we say we are in the religious service of God.' What was simply religious service in holy places, on holy days, by holy people in those Old Testament times, has now have been succeeded and replaced by the amazing privilege of the service of the ministry of God in the spread of the good news of Jesus. That is what it is. That's worship.

Just as we saw on Monday that everything we do as Christian people in this world is by way of being worship; in the particular matter of being led by God in a particular line of service, that too is worship. The old religious doings have all been replaced by this wonderful fact: my whole life and your whole life in the service of the Lord Jesus Christ is, day by day, hour by hour, the worship of God.

Sanctification These Gentile converts, an offering acceptable to God, are being sanctified by the Holy Spirit. What I called 'theology' is the great over-arching, under-girding gospel of God which has sent the apostle Paul to them. 'Worship' is what they find themselves brought into, a life of worship as they respond to His gospel. And 'sanctification' is what happens to them then. To put it another way, wherever Paul went it was the principles of the gospel that directed, guided, led and controlled him; that's theology. Whatever Paul did he saw as ministry, the true translation into New Testament terms of Old Testament religion, the equivalent of the Old Testament priesthood; that's worship. And whoever he met and served in this way, he saw in his converts the potential to become God's holy people; and that's sanctification.

Paul is, of course, a very special case. His way, in the sense of the route he followed and the travels through which God led him, is not our way. None of us is likely to be led from Jerusalem all the way round to Illyricum and back again and then off to Rome and Spain as pioneer evangelists—because none of us is called to be an apostle of Jesus Christ in the sense that Paul was, let alone called to be that particular apostle, in those circumstances, with that particular task. Paul's way, in the sense of the route by which God led him, was Paul's alone. But the way that God led him in the sense of the methods by which God led him—that is for all of us; it's from that that we have to learn.

The way that God leads us

You'll see how God's coincidences bring us to the end of Romans 15, immediately after the evening of our World View service and the call of God to men and women to serve Him in many other places[1]. Here we arrive at a Bible passage which treats of that very subject.

---

1. See p. 161 in the present volume.

Theology

Look again at verse 16 and the phrase 'the gospel of God', which is theology. The gospel is not merely the message—though it is that. Still less is merely the proclaiming of the message—though it is that. The gospel is the whole framework within which God leads His people.

God's plan Some of you will remember that grand old hymn book *Golden Bells*. I well remember its opening section, before anything more explicitly dealing with the gospel, headed 'Creation, providence and grace'. That is part of the gospel, that the God of creation, providence and grace has set up the whole scheme. There is nothing in the whole grand plan that is deserved, even by the apostle Paul, let alone by us! Every single thing in the whole plan has been meticulously planned before the worlds began, by the God of creation, providence and grace.

This is as true of us as it was for Paul; that by the God of creation, providence and grace, all His servants have been prepared for good works which He has planned beforehand, that they should walk in. The God of providence has prepared His servants by the background He has given to each of them. Their ancestry, the family they came from, the place they were born, the way they were brought up, the education He provided for them—the God of providence has been seeing to all of that. He has prepared all His servants, the apostles and us alike, by the gifts He has given to us, the experiences He brings our way, the characters He forms within us, the opportunities He sets before us. The great God of providence who loves us and wants to bless others through us as well, has been busily at work. All these things are part of the gospel. And He has instilled into every one of His servants the two great fundamental responses.

How profound are those initial words of our Lord and Saviour Jesus Christ as reported by Mark. Jesus comes on to the scene in the gospel story with these words: 'Repent and believe' (Mark 1:15). That's what it's all about. If we are His people, the God of providence has brought us through all those long years of preparation—our background, culture, family, birth, upbringing and education—to this point. He says, 'Now there are just two things that I require of you; that you repent and believe. And that repeatedly and incessantly, all the way through your Christian life and all the way through your service of the gospel, you come back to Me again and again in repentance, and day by day you say, "God be merciful to me a sinner." And that repeatedly and incessantly you come back to Me in Christ and say, "Lord, I hand over my life to You, You know best how to run it, You know the way You want to lead me, it is all to be Your guidance, Your leading, Your way, Your principles." '

That repeated daily hatred of sin, that repeated daily clinging to God—that's gospel theology. It is the framework for every possible question of guidance. Do you see how it takes us back to chapter 12? We mentioned the seventy possible meanings of the phrase 'the measure of faith' in Romans 12:3, and I told you the one that I am convinced is the right one; faith is the measure, the old original simple faith of the sinner returning to God. God says, 'Use that as your measure in every circumstance every day of your lives. Whenever questions about My leading arise, whenever a choice of opportunities opens before you, whenever it seems that I may be saying, "Go this way," or "Go that way," come back with that simple response of repentance and faith.'

Faith as the measure, an ever-deeper awareness of the deceitfulness of your own heart and an ever-greater confidence of the loving providence of God. Those are the basic, fundamental twin principles, not only of Christian living, but also of Christian leading. And it's that gospel theology which shapes all our understanding of God's will.

God's will   The actual phrase appears in 15:31–32. 'Pray that I may be rescued'—he's speaking about his return to Jerusalem from the unbelievers in Judaea—'and that my service in Jerusalem may be acceptable to the saints there, so that by God's will'—at last he comes to it—'I may come to you with joy and together with you be refreshed.'

I pricked up my ears when in our World View service we heard about God's will in its differing senses, the general will of God and the specific will of God, for I wrote those words in my own notes for these Bible Readings a couple of weeks ago.

God's *general will* for His people is what we know He wants; the things which, He has made perfectly clear in Scripture, His people are to obey. There is no question whatever about the general will of God. 'These are the things you don't do,' He says. 'These are the laws that still apply even to Christian people. This is the way of life. Law is never the way *to* life, but law as the way *of* life says there are things you don't do.' And there are the things you are to do. There is no question about the things that God hates and about the things that God wants. That is His general will.

It is very interesting that it's in the context of that general will of God that Paul the apostle, who knows the mind of God so well, feels perfectly free to talk about his ambitions. 'I have a great ambition to come to Rome,' he says, 'I have a great longing to see you in Rome.' Is it God's will? I wonder, might God be leading him in a different way?—Paul doesn't seem to care about that. He is so rooted and grounded in his knowledge of what God does and does not want that he feels perfectly free to say, 'I'd love to do that . . . No, I don't think I'll do that . . . I think maybe I'll go over here and I won't go over there.' That very human reaction to circumstances is perfectly allowable, it seems, in the heart and mind of a man who knows deep down and practises daily the things that he knows God does want. In other words, his is a holy life, a life of repentance and trust; within that, he lays his own plans.

One of the great and dangerous sayings of Augustine, whom I have already quoted in these Bible Readings, is '*Ama et fac quod vis*—Love [God] and do what you like.'

'You can't mean that,' you say.

Oh yes!—when you understand it as Augustine understood it. If you love God, if your heart is daily right with Him, if you know clearly the general will of God and the things that He disallows and the things that He fosters, if you know that you are living daily by those principles—then you can do what you like and you are free to make plans, to go to Rome and to Spain, to go back to Jerusalem first, or whatever it may be. And God will bless you if your heart is right with Him. That is the general will of God.

God's *specific will* turns out to be 'what actually happened'—which Paul didn't know beforehand. It's very interesting that Paul had some ideas as to what he would like to do. He said, 'I would like to go to Jerusalem, and I hope you will pray with me, that I may be rescued from the unbelievers there, and that I will come to see you in Rome.' I wonder if God said with a twinkle in His eye, 'That is exactly what *will* happen, though not at all in the way you think.' For it was exactly what happened. He went to Jerusalem. He was about to be lynched by the mob, was rescued from the hands of the unbelievers, was put into custody and went to Rome as a prisoner. I've often thought how very often, for example throughout the book of Judges, God says, 'You know perfectly well that I am going to rescue My believing people. They put their trust in Me, I'll rescue them. But how I do it is another matter.' And the method of God's working in the book of Judges is repeatedly, totally unexpected. *What* He does, you know from His general will. *How* He does it is a different matter and never ceases to surprise His people.

Worship

There's a lot about worship in verse 16 and the surrounding verses. Verses 15–16: 'The grace'—that's a religious word—'to be a minister'—that's a religious word—'. . . with the priestly duty'—that's a religious word—'. . . so that the Gentiles might become an offering acceptable to God'—that's a religious expression; all those words are religious.

Verse 27: 'For if the Gentiles have shared in the Jews' spiritual blessings, they owe it to the Jews to share with them [AV: to minister to them] their material blessings.' The word 'minister' is the same as in verse 16. Paul is saying, 'My service of the gospel is the equivalent of the Old Testament temple ministry. But it's not mine alone as an apostle, because all those delightful Gentile churches in Macedonia and Achaia are involved in the same religious ministry. In the old days it would have been a priest in a temple offering animals for slaughter. Nowadays it's Gentile Christians putting money in a collection. That's priestly ministry, the ministry of the temple. It's all worship. They are all religious terms, but transmuted into an entire way of Christian life and service.'

As we've seen, we tend to enclose these things once again in religion. We lift them out of Old Testament religion and we put them back into a religious box in our New Testament days. That's not the right way to do it, though it's almost impossible not to. Here are all these complex structures of Old Testament worship reproduced in supposedly Christian garb, in what we call New Testament worship. And it's true that the New Testament does expect Christian people to get together for the kind of things we do on Sundays in church buildings.

When I was first ordained, my vicar, Fred Pickering at Christ Church Southport, told me that he had one requirement, and only one, of his curates. I thought he was about to lay before me a whole spectrum curatorial duties. 'No,' he said. 'I just want you to do one thing, I want you to memorise the General Exhortation at the beginning of Morning and Evening Prayer, in the Book of Common Prayer.'

Those of you who worship in Anglican churches will know the Exhortation. It speaks about those times . . .

> . . . when we assemble and meet together to render thanks for the great benefits that we have received at his hands, to set forth his most worthy praise, to hear his most holy Word, and to ask those things which are requisite and necessary, as well for the body as for soul.

And the New Testament tells us to come together: 'Not forsaking the assembling of ourselves together, as the manner of some is' (Heb. 10:25, AV). It is an important part of Christian life that you come together at the most convenient time and the most convenient place, to do that kind of thing.

But that is not the equivalent of Old Testament worship. The real counterpart to Old Testament worship is what Paul is speaking about in Romans 15. It is our service of the gospel. It is going out into the world to spread the news of Jesus. The real equivalent of those Old Testament religious doings is the service, not the services; the service of weekdays, not the service of Sundays. That is what worship is, into which God leads His people.

Sanctification

Lastly, the 'offering' of the Gentiles (that religious term in verse 16) is to be sanctified by the Holy Spirit. This again is the way that God leads us, on the basis of that grand theology, into a whole life of worship. Its object is sanctification.

I want as I close to point out two notable things about Paul's use of the term 'sanctified' in 15:16.

Paul is not talking about his own sanctification   Here is a message central to the Keswick Convention. We come here to think in our own hearts about how we ourselves ought to be living a sanctified life. That is very important, and one of the crucial things that Keswick is about. But what Paul is speaking about here is not his own sanctification but the sanctification of those he serves. And in all matters of leading and guidance, by all means we must think about how we ourselves should be moving forward in sanctification, the process by which we ourselves become more and more like Jesus. But Paul says, 'I want you to look beyond that, and think also about the sanctification of those who will be blessed through you.'

It is something we should have in mind in all that we seek to do for Him, so that our Christian faith and service is preserved from self-centredness, is always looking outwards, to say, 'Lord, how can So-and-so be blessed? You bless me endlessly, but how can So-and-so be blessed? I want to grow more like You—but how can I help someone else to grow more like You? Sanctification in my own heart is a thing I aim at constantly, but Oh! I would love to see Joe Bloggs sanctified, and Mary Snooks sanctified, and all the difficult people in my church sanctified. My great aim, the object of my prayers, is their sanctification, in every opportunity and situation that opens up before us.'

Will it be my delight not simply to become like Christ myself, but to minister to others in such a way that they are sanctified too? That's what Paul has in mind here as he uses the word 'sanctified'.

This is not Paul's normal use of the word 'sanctification' Paul almost always uses 'sanctification' as most of us would probably use the word. We are talking about the process that I spoke of earlier, the process of becoming more and more like Jesus—a growth in holiness. That is how Paul usually uses the word. But here he uses it as the book of Hebrews tends to use it, with a slightly different meaning. Like Romans 15:16, the letter to the Hebrews is steeped in all the religious terms of the Old Testament faith. And in Hebrews, 'sanctification' tends to mean much more: not the process, but the point at the outset when something is taken hold of by God and is turned round to be directed towards Him. God says, 'From this day forward that thing, that person, is holy to Me. In the Pauline sense, that person may have a very long way yet to go in becoming holy. But I have set My label upon him, upon her, from this moment forward.' And as the inner life becomes more and more like Jesus, from the very outset that person has become, in the Hebrews sense, sanctified. 'It is labelled as Mine,' says the Lord. And in that most unusual way for him, Paul uses the word here to mean the initial setting apart that begins the process.

It is in fact the equivalent of conversion. It is the setting of our path in the right direction. It is repentance and trust all the way through. Paul says, 'That is the way God leads me.' And he would say to us, 'That is the way God will lead you too. You have made that initial turn, many years ago maybe. You were sanctified, set in the right direction. And now you are being sanctified in that right direction.'

I want you to pray that for yourselves and for others, and for all those to whom God will send us and lead us.

5: The Love We Are To Share
Romans 16:1–27

Romans is a hugely influential book of the Bible. But I suspect we often think that its greatness lies in those early chapters: chapters 1–8 certainly, probably chapters 1–11, perhaps even chapters 1–15. And once Paul starts on his lengthy list of greetings, we tend to think it's not quite so important or valuable as what has gone before.

One of the many paradoxes we have encountered in Romans this week is that in chapter 16 you have a list of real, flesh-and-blood people who were known in those first-century fellowships; yet somehow these real people are less real to us than the teaching of chapters 1–15. The people are dead, it is the doctrine and the application that live.

Well, I believe that there's as much living truth in these lists of names as there is in the rest of Romans! And I hope that this last study together in Paul's closing chapter will demonstrate that for us.

I want to make three points as we begin.

Chapter 16 is not just a list of names Even the names are not merely names. We can learn a lot from them. And there are certainly many names in the first sixteen verses, but the list gives way in verse 17 to a set of warnings that we will need to consider as our second section. Then a list follows of Paul's companions in Corinth from whence we believe he was writing. This leads to Paul's doxology, beginning at verse 25.

We will meet Paul's friends one day   Have you ever had some-body button-hole you, and you know them fairly well, but they want to make sure you know them better? They start telling you about their sons, daughters, daughters-in-law, sons-in-law, un-cles and aunts and grandchildren—and all in great detail—until your head is spinning. So in your confusion, you switch off. But later you meet one those relatives about whom you are now supposed to know everything. And you realise in great embar-rassment that you didn't pay attention as you should have done when you had the chance.

We have an obligation to pay attention to Romans 16, because one day we shall be meeting all these people. I'm quite sure that when we get to heaven we will certainly know one another. But I believe that we shall also know everyone else. All God's people from the whole of Bible history, and indeed the whole of history—every one who belongs to the Lord Jesus Christ. We won't know them less well, we'll know them infinitely better when we get there; and we'll have them all to meet. How embarrassing if people don't know what to say to them! The information was there all the time, we ought to have known.

My father very much liked one of the modern translations of a phrase in verse 9: 'Dear old Stachys'. Stachys is a real friend whom we shall meet again. Handley Moule in his commentary writes, 'We watch this unknown yet well-beloved company with a sense of fellowship and expectation impossible out of Christ. This page is no mere relic of the past, it is a list of friendships to be made hereafter.' How about that!

So let's pay attention to these folk whom we'll be meeting one day. We shall certainly know them then, but it would be rather nice to get to know them now; and it will sharpen our anticipa-tion of heaven. Paul has already told us in chapter 13 that the day is at hand, the night is far spent; before we realise it we shall be there, meeting Priscilla and Aquila and Epenetus and all the rest of them.

What kind of fellowships is Paul describing?   However, there is a more important question than who these people were: what kind of fellowships are they that are described in this chapter? For though we may not know these people personally now, we certainly know fellowships of this type. We can extrapolate from the kind of groups and churches that they belonged to back into our own situation, and find all sorts of valuable lessons. What they were applies immediately to what we are, and to what our fellowships are. The churches in Corinth from which the letter was sent and in Rome to which it was sent have been reflected repeatedly down through Christian history. We have much to learn from them that we can apply to our own Christian fellowships today.

So though these dear folk are dead, like Abel they yet speak (cf. Heb. 11:4). It is not only the doctrines of Romans 1–11 that are alive, and the application of that doctrine in chapters 12–15 that is a living word from God, but also these greetings from the apostle to his friends who in one sense are long dust just as he is, yet are nevertheless a living truth for us today. And I hope we shall find it so.

Paul's friends: the joy of a wide fellowship (16:1–16)

There are thirty-five names in this chapter. The first is that of Phoebe, Paul's postwoman. We're not quite sure what she is—'a servant of the church in Cenchrea'—maybe she's a deaconess. Or perhaps it simply means she is a very helpful member, serving others in the church in Cenchrea. Which ever it is, she's certainly going to be very helpful to Paul and to the church in Rome who will be receiving by her hand the letter that he's writing to them.

After Phoebe we have twenty-six names of Christians in the city of Rome, from verse 3 down to verse 16. Twenty-six is actually a misleading figure. For example, 'those who belong to the household of Aristobulus' and 'those in the household of Narcissus who are in the Lord' (verses 10–11) may possibly not include either of those two men, who could have been rich pagans with no profession of Christianity but in whose household were Christian representatives. They may have been numerous. Even if Aristobulus was not a Christian, he could have had a whole fleet of converted people working away underground in his household, praying for the conversion of their master, and the same goes for the household of Narcissus.

There are others around. Verse 5 speaks of the church that meets in the house of Priscilla and Aquila; verse 14, 'the brothers with them' (that is, Asyncritus and his friends); verse 15, 'all the saints with them'. So there are numerous other people. Rufus' mother (verse 13) is not given a name, but she's a real person. Nereus' sister (verse 15) is not given a name, but she's a real person. So the church in Rome is not just twenty-six individuals. They are more than that. That is who they are.

But as I have said, much more to our purpose this morning is *what* they are. I want to say four things about this wide fellowship of Paul's friends in Rome.

It was a Christian fellowship

This goes without saying; we know it from the very beginning of the letter. Romans 1:7 tells us that Paul is writing 'to all in Rome who are loved by God and called to be saints'. And he specifies on a number of occasions in this list So-and-So 'who is in Christ', somebody else 'who is in the Lord', 'the saints' who are in their house; crowds of folk who form a Christian fellowship.

It was an active fellowship

Priscilla and Aquila risked their necks to save Paul's life (cf verse 4). 'My dear friend Epenetus'—the first fruits for Christ, and other fruit has followed from him. 'Tryphena and Tryphosa, those women who work hard in the Lord . . . and Persis, another woman who has worked very hard in the Lord . . . and [Rufus'] mother, who has been a mother to me, too . . .' These are people who are busily active in Christian service, fervent in the Spirit, 'serving the Lord', as it says back in 12:11.

Then, perhaps even more significantly,

It was a Roman fellowship

Not in the sense that all these people were necessarily born in Rome, but that they were living there at the time. Why is it significant that the fellowship to which Paul writes is a Roman fellowship? How is that fellowship like ours? What do we learn from the fact that it was in Rome? I doubt if many in the tent this morning live in Italy. That can't be the connection.

But they were a Christian group living in a big city. Now *that* might be like where quite a number of us live; a big important city where many people come and go; with great opportunities, among many who don't yet know the Lord, for the spread of the gospel. That might be it. But that's not what I have in mind.

Rome was certainly a big city and therefore a strategic place. From Rome roads went out in all directions across the empire. What opportunities for the service of Christ! And many of us live not simply in big cities but in strategic cities. It may be that you say, 'Well I live out in the country,' but you may know that too is a very strategic place to be, and there's very worthwhile service to give to the Lord in your village, in your rural area, wherever it may be. But it's not actually the strategic nature of Rome, any more than its urban character, that I have in mind.

Why is it important that this letter was sent to a Roman fellowship? It's obvious when you come to think of it. *The Roman fellowship was the one that received the letter to the Romans.* This was that privileged fellowship, the first of all the Christian churches down through Christian history who were able to open this letter and read, 'Paul, a servant of Christ Jesus, called to be an apostle and set apart for the gospel of God' and so on through the wonderful things that we've been looking at during this week. This was the fellowship that first received this letter.

It is not an easy book. Some new-ish Christians, knowing that you're supposed to read the Bible, open it dutifully at page 1, work their way through Genesis and get bogged down in Leviticus. Some then say, 'I can't make head or tail of Leviticus. I'll start at the back'—and they instantly get bogged down in Revelation. If they then choose to open the Bible three-quarters of the way through and find themselves in Romans, well—it's a wonderful book, but if you're new to this sort of thing it can be pretty daunting too.

Yet you and I are well aware that if you dig into this letter you will find it a gold mine. I hope that my congregation five or six years ago at St Nicholas', Durham, to whom I preached thirty-three sermons on the letter to the Romans, weren't politely

concealing the fact that they were flagging at the end! I hope that
they were not deterred but enthused by Romans and found it, as
I believe you found it, a wonderful letter.

Now, here is the fellowship that heard Paul's letter to the
Romans before anyone else ever did. Could we come to it with
that freshness? We've heard about Romans before. But suppose
you never had? Suppose as an eager, enthusiastic young Christian you opened up that letter and began to see the gospel of
Christ opened out before you by that master expositor, the
apostle Paul? That's a great thing for any Christian fellowship to
try to recapture: to open up this letter and say, 'Lord, make it
fresh to me.'

It was a wide fellowship

I don't mean just that there are lots of names. My question, and
probably yours too, is this. We know from chapter 15 that Paul
had not yet visited Rome. So how come that he knew so many
people in a city that he had never been to? Again, Handley
Moule has something to say on this. 'Many students of this
epistle,' says the good bishop, 'find a serious difficulty in this list
of friends so placed. The person so familiar, the place so strange.
And they would have us look on this sixteenth chapter as a
fragment from some other letter, pieced in here by mistake.'

That's what some commentators would tell us, but I like that
little phrase, 'the person so familiar, the place so strange.' A few
years ago I visited Australia. And I took greetings from my
parents, to David, Margaret, Robert, Sheila, John and Chris, in
the city of Sydney. But Mum and Dad had never been to
Australia. How did they know all these people? It's obvious, isn't
it. They were English friends of theirs who had left England and
were now living in that great cosmopolitan city on the other side
of the world. That was how Paul knew so many people in a city
he had never visited. Rome was like that! All sorts of people went
to Rome. Many of Paul's friends whom he'd met in other places
were now in Rome, and so he could send his greetings to a wide
fellowship gathered from all over.

It's not simply the longest of Paul's lists of names. It's the
most extensive as well. Many Christian people have a world-

wide correspondence with friends they've made here and there and who've now travelled and are far away. You keep in touch, if only at Christmas. Or maybe, still better, you keep a world-wide prayer list, and your prayers fly to and fro, pursuing folk who once lived in the same town and belonged to the same congregation that you did, and are now in other countries far away. A wide fellowship! And what stands out for me in verses 1–16 is, what a joy it is—and what a Keswick kind of thing it is; 'All one in Christ Jesus'[1]. It is not simply that all of us who are gathered here might, for all we know, come from just down the road, and we are all one in Christ Jesus. In fact we have come from a very widely scattered area from many parts of the world. We are 'all one in Christ Jesus' in the sense of being that sort of extensive fellowship, part of the universal church of Jesus Christ. That's a joy, and it's a very Keswick kind of thing.

Do you know that great hymn of Heaven, 'Ten thousand times ten thousand'? It says of our arrival in that other world,

> O then what raptured greetings
> on Canaan's happy shore,
> What knitting severed friendships up,
> where partings are no more![2] (*Henry Alford*)

But we can have a foretaste of that in this world. Even before we find all the severed friendships knitted up on that other shore, we know that we have it here. There are all sorts of connections in this wonderful network, the wide fellowship of the Christian church. I hope you enjoy that as I do. I hope you make friendships here that will continue when we are sundered far from one another.

Paul's warnings: the importance of a united fellowship (16:17–20)

We come now to a little passage of warning about the importance of a united fellowship.

---

1. Gal. 3:28 the Keswick motto (*Ed.*).
2. In some modern hymnbooks this stanza is omitted, for no obvious reason (*Ed.*).

What is practical holy living?

This has been his concern from chapter 12 onwards. Now in verse 19 he gives a very good description of what he means. 'I want you to be wise about what is good, and innocent about what is evil' (16:19). Practical holiness means being wise about what is good and doing it, and being innocent about what is evil and not doing that.

It's an understanding of what right living, what holiness, is. Of course it is vital that at the beginning of our Christian experience the gospel should touch our hearts. But woe betide the Christian whose faith is confined only to his heart and never touches his mind! Paul says, 'I want you to be wise, I want you to be understanding. I want intelligent Christians who have an educated grasp of what the gospel is.' It's quite true that there are all too many Christians who have the gospel in their heads and never let it down into their hearts; but it is equally possible for Christians to have the gospel in their hearts and never to let it ascend to their heads—unintelligent, uneducated Christians who are happy to be uninstructed and never to get beyond the first grade—that is a bad thing. 'I want you to be wise about what is good; I want you have an educated grasp of the worthwhile things, of what is involved in the practice of holy living. That's the only way you're going to do it; by knowing what you are supposed to be doing.'

'On the other hand,' says Paul, 'I want you to be innocent about what is evil.' In the previous verse, you'll see in the NIV, Paul has used the word 'naïve'. By that he means something quite different to what he means by 'innocent' in verse 19. The book of Proverbs teaches us in what spiritual danger we are in if we are naïve . 'But I do want you to be innocent'—that is to say, having a gospel that has touched both your heart and your mind you know then what to do about both good and evil; and the things that are bad you deliberately, knowingly, intelligently and educatedly keep away from. You will keep yourself free from contamination: that's what he means by innocence. 'Free from the contamination of what you know to be evil, you will allow it no foothold in your life, you will follow the example of the Lord Jesus Christ when he says, "The prince of this world is coming.

He has no hold on me" (John 14:30). "There is nothing in my personality," says Jesus, "that Satan can get a purchase on." And I want you to be the same, innocent with respect to what is evil. Knowingly innocent, knowingly uncontaminated. Don't give it a place, don't give Satan a foothold or a handhold.'

'I want you to be wise about what is good, and innocent about what is evil.' Paul is putting into that one phrase the whole of Romans 12 to 15. His theme is the practice of holy living.

What will Satan do to try to spoil it?
He is afraid that Satan will try to spoil it. It's true that in the end (verse 20), 'The God of peace will soon crush Satan under your feet.' But in the meantime people within your fellowships will come in and Satan will use them to cause real problems. They are people who bring not simply obstacles for Christians to trip over, also but divisions (cf verse 17).

I find it very interesting that Paul warns that Satan will attempt to thwart those who are trying to live a practical holy life, using his servants who come disguised into Christian fellowships and cause divisions. You see, he is assuming that the practice of holy living means growing up in a fellowship, that he is not speaking to isolated, individualist Christians. If you are going to practise holy living, he says, you must be doing it in fellowship; because he identifies one of the great dangers that might spoil your attempts towards holy living, and it is divisions in the fellowship. John Wesley said, 'The Bible knows nothing of solitary religion.' The assumption throughout is that even if you find some of the fellowships to which you belong really difficult, fellowship—somehow, somewhere—you must have. It is in a group, a congregation, a network of Christian friends, a church, a fellowship, that the apostle envisages growth in practical Christian holiness.

There may of course be other reasons why we may find ourselves in a particular fellowship.

We may be there because *God has called us to serve there.* You may be a minister in a church where you feel yourself sometimes to be the only one who is serving the Lord, but you believe God has put you there for His service. You are not finding fellowship in your own congregation. I believe that you should—I'm opposed to the old idea that a minister must only find friends in other places and not in his own congregation. But it may be that you have to look elsewhere because there is simply nobody that you resonate with.

We may be there because *God wants us there to witness to Him*. There's not much going on in that fellowship, but He's put you there for that purpose.

We may be there because *there's no alternative*. You live right out in the sticks and it's the only church there is. Well now, God knows all about that. But God still says to you that for yourself and your own health's good, then somewhere, somehow—even if it's not there, it must be somewhere else—you must find fellowship. It is there that practical holy living will grow.

What precautions can we take against it being spoiled?
Paul's advice is to work away at the principles that he has been setting before us. He wants practical holy living. He is afraid that it may be spoiled for us by divisions in our fellowship, so his advice is, work away at these principles.

In verse 18 we saw the negative: naïvety. The great positive is in verse 19: obedience. 'Let's not have any naïve Christians,' he says. 'I want your mind to be engaged in this.'

Charles Cranfield comments drily on Romans 16:18, 'Paul was realistic enough to recognise that Christians are very often quite as far from being as wise as serpents as they are from being harmless as doves.' You must put your mind to it. If your mind is engaged, you will be guarding against that great negative force of naïvety, of being a Christian simpleton, a stupid Christian. Don't be one! Get your mind to work.

So in verse 19, Paul says, 'I'm glad you've got the great positive, obedience. Everyone's heard about your obedience. I'm full of joy over you. It means that your will is engaged. When God sets before you His commands, you say, "I will do that, my mind has grasped the things to avoid and my will is set on the things to cultivate." '

And what is it to which we have to put our mind and will? Verse 17: 'I urge you, brothers, to watch out for those who cause divisions and put obstacles in your way that are contrary to the teaching you have learned.' What you have to put your mind and will to, says Paul, is the letter to the Romans, the things you've learned, the things I've been teaching you in the last fifteen chapters, and all that goes along with that: the whole of the rest of Scripture surrounding this wonderful letter. 'But that,' he says, 'is where I want you to engage your heart and mind and will: the importance of a united fellowship based upon, gathered together around, the truth of the gospel as I have been setting it out before you,' says the apostle.

Paul's companions: the value of a close fellowship (16:21–24)

Notice that verse 24 only exists in a few manuscripts. In the NIV it's included as a footnote. So we'll look at verses 21–23 and go on to verse 25.

Our next section speaks about Paul's companions, who are his friends in Corinth from where he is writing. It's another list of names; there are eight mentioned. Just like verses 1–16? Well, it's not quite the same kind of list. What makes the difference is the close fellowship gathered around Paul as he writes. These people are identified more closely than those at the beginning of the chapter; so much so that we can make an educated guess as to who they are.

A close fellowship

Timothy, of course, we know. He appears in many other places in the New Testament, this wonderful young fellow whom Paul knew from his earliest days; a great friend of the family.

Next Lucius, Jason and Sosipater. Lucius may be the 'Lucius of Cyrene' who appears in Acts 13:1. He'd come from Antioch and Paul met him very early on in the days of his ministry. He'd actually come from much further afield. He was Lucius of Cyrene, he'd come over from North Africa, to Syria, to Antioch, and now here he is in Corinth, if it's the same Lucius. Jason is perhaps the Jason who lived in Thessalonica (cf Acts 17). If you've got a geographical turn of mind you will see that I'm tracing one of those arcs around the Eastern Mediterranean.

Lucius, from Antioch maybe; Jason, from Thessalonica maybe. There was a Sopater in Berea, a little bit further into Greece. I wonder if that was where Paul picked him up? But in all events here they are, the three of them together now, in Corinth.

Then Tertius and Gaius, Erastus and Quartus. It's a fair guess that they were all local Corinth residents, members of the local church.

Now, even if those guesses are not all correct, nevertheless these people can be identified considerably more closely than those in the first sixteen verses.

A close relationship

But there's more to this list than that. These eight people seem to have had a close relationship. Not just because they were all in Corinth, not even because they all presumably turned up at the house of Gaius once in a while. Have you noticed how often the little word 'my' comes in these three verses? There were connections, there were relationships, and Paul can write of Timothy, his 'fellow worker'. If he had had the space and inclination he could have said much more about Timothy, his beloved son in the faith, his convert, his right-hand man.

Lucius, Jason and Sosipater were his 'relatives'. Tertius was his secretary. Gaius, in whose house Paul was staying as he wrote the letter, was his host. Erastus, of course was an important person; he was the city's director of public works. Mandarins of the civil service don't often make close friendships, do they? But Erastus was a brother in Christ, and so was Quartus, who was of course a much humbler sort of person. I wonder what is meant by 'Quartus our brother'. Paul actually just says 'brother Quartus', and the commentators have made all sorts of guesses as to what he means by that. Was he just a Christian brother? But then so were all the rest of them. Was he actually related to Paul? I don't think it's that either. Here's a suggestion I haven't found in any of the commentaries. 'Tertius' means 'third', 'Quartus' means 'fourth'. Were Tertius' parents rather unimaginative people, and did they perhaps have four sons, and was Quartus Tertius' kid brother, therefore put last? Paul has listed all the other names, and there's Quartus: 'Me too, me too!'—so Quartus gets put in as well.

But aren't they close relationships? Relationships within a family, relationships within the work, relationships where you live, the friends you stay with; lovely close fellowship, and very valuable to Paul as he writes.

A close interest

They must have had a close interest in what was going on. We can imagine these eight people, in and out of the house of Gaius, who was obviously quite well-to-do. He was not only Paul's host, he was the host of the whole church. Maybe the church used to meet in Gaius' big house. There were always folk in and out of that house, and they all knew that up there in the prophet's chamber Paul was busy writing the letter. And they'd put their heads around the door; and somebody would ask if they could take the coffee and biscuits up half-way through the morning, and they'd go up and say, 'Hello Paul, how are you getting on? Chapter 7? Oh, that's difficult, isn't it.' I do wonder whether that close interest was always helpful! You know the kind of dedication you sometimes see in books — 'To my wife and children, without whom this book would have been written a great deal more quickly than it was' . . .

It must surely have been a thrilling thing to be in the fellowship described in section 1, to be in the Roman congregation when the letter arrived, to be the first readers ever of Romans. But perhaps it was even more thrilling to have been the little group who gathered round while it was being written, as Paul was mulling over how he would phrase this or put that, as he tried it out on whoever happened to be in the room at the time. 'I want to say this, does it make sense to you?' It must have been a great thrill.

So here is a group of companions, not just friends, with Paul. A group of Christian friends, closely involved with Paul and with one another, for the whole time it took for that wonderful letter to get written, before Phoebe was eventually sent off to deliver it to Rome.

The joys of Keswick, be it Convention Week or Holiday Week, happen once a year. They bring about a gathering together of a wide fellowship from all parts of the country and of the world, and that occasional wide fellowship is something very special. But I'm sure you recognise as I do, and value as I try to do, the ongoing regular fellowship of the group back home; where the people come and go, and you meet them most days, and you know their difficulties and their problems, and the traits that exasperate and irritate you. But that's the fellowship where you belong. Paul's companions show us something of that, as it was in his day in the city of Corinth. And it shows us the same sort of thing which likewise applies in our own day—the value of a close fellowship, and how we are to seek it, foster it and make the very most of it.

Paul's doxology: the strength of a gospel fellowship (16:25–27)

So this tremendous letter comes to an end. Mind you, it came to an end in 11:33, and in 15:13, and in 15:33, and in 16:20! Paul keeps thinking of things to add. But this really is the end, and 16:25–27 is his closing doxology for the entire letter.

Not everybody agrees that this is actually Paul's own doxology. Somebody else may have written it and added it at the end. But even if so, it certainly sums up all the thinking and the teaching of the apostle Paul throughout this letter.

He speaks about the letter, but it's not just a letter. He calls it 'my gospel', the proclamation of Jesus Christ, the revelation of the mystery. I have quoted already from the good things I love in the Book of Common Prayer. But I don't think everything is marvellous in the Prayer Book. And I have always thought it rather odd that there is a distinction made in the Communion Service between the reading of the Gospel and the reading of the Epistle; that everybody is required to stand for the Gospel but not for the Epistle. Sometimes I think, 'But the whole thing is gospel, isn't it?' And if I am reading Romans 16:25–27, it's all gospel.

Paul's letter
How does Paul describe this letter of his which is the gospel?

The gospel was hidden for long ages past (16:25). He is speaking of the Old Testament—all those hundreds of years, and all those many, many books written in the course of them, in which, though it was clear what God was going to do, it was not clear how He would do it. I've made that distinction before. All through the Old Testament the matter is hidden, in the sense that you know that God is the great Saviour who is going to rescue His people; but you don't know how. You have glimmerings and inklings and pointers, but in a sense it's a mystery hidden for long ages past.

But the gospel is now revealed (16:26). Now he is speaking of the New Testament. That's when it all comes out into the open, and you realise what the mystery hidden in the Old Testament is actually all about: God manifested in the flesh. It all becomes real. Jesus opens to us in all the Scriptures, things concerning Himself. It all comes out into the open, and we see.

The gospel is made known through the prophetic writings by the command of the eternal God, so that all nations might believe and obey him (16:26). Now he speaks of the whole of Scripture, which is for the proclamation and response through the whole world. That is the gospel. All that was written in old times, now made plain to us in Jesus, is there in order to be proclaimed throughout the nations for people to respond to it.

Paul's readers
Paul's readers are the people in Corinth reading the letter over his shoulder as they watched it being written, the people in Rome who listened to the reading of it, and all God's people ever since, everywhere, including ourselves. Paul says to us, his readers, 'You know what this is for, don't you; you know why I've written all this? It is, in the terms of verse 25, to establish you by my gospel.'

How strong is that local fellowship, when it is a gospel fellowship! How strong is the whole church of Christ, when it is seen to be squarely based upon this gospel! That's the strength of a gospel fellowship, in which you and I and all our fellow believers are established in the truths we've been studying.

That's what the doxology says about the letter and about the readers. Finally it says something about the Lord, who through the mouth of His apostle spoke this Scripture, and by the pen of His apostle wrote this Scripture; the Lord who called His church and builds it and equips it and makes it holy by this Scripture.

'To the only wise God be glory for ever through Jesus Christ! Amen.'

'Pattern for Godliness'
Deuteronomy 5:1–21

by Rev. Stuart Briscoe

1: Deuteronomy 5:1–7

A number of years ago, in our church in Milwaukee, we went into the market and other places where people congregate and interviewed them on the subject of the Ten Commandments. We asked them, 'Do you believe that the Ten Commandments are important?' Without exception, they said, 'Oh, yes.' Then we asked, 'What is your favourite Commandment?', which produced some fascinating answers. A very striking finding emerged from our research. Every person interviewed thought that the Ten Commandments were appropriate and significant and most said they lived their lives by them. But they had extreme difficulty in telling us what they were.

Thus it's always appropriate for us to go back to these fundamental truths of the Scriptures, because sometimes we tend to take them for granted and we are not always sure what they are actually saying.

It is absolutely imperative to read in context. A 'text' out of its 'context' is a 'con', and this can lead to great confusion. In the deep south of America, an old man was walking along with his mule and his hunting dog when a pick-up truck knocked all three into the ditch. The man sued the driver, whose lawyer tried in court to argue that there was nothing wrong with the man. In fact, said the lawyer, at the time of the incident the man had said that he 'never felt better in his life'. He cross-examined the plaintiff.

'Did my client come to you after the alleged accident, and did he ask you if you were all right?'

'Yes.'

'And did you reply, "I have never felt better in my life"?'

''Well,' said the old man, 'Me and my mule and my dog were walking along and this man came round the corner too fast, and he knocked us into the ditch. He jumped out of the cab with his shotgun. He went to my dog, and it was bleeding so he shot it. He went to my mule and its foreleg was broken so he shot it. Finally he asked me, "Are you all right?" And I said, "I've never felt better in my life.". . .'

The moral is, we must read our passage today in context.

Introduction

Before we study the Commandments individually, I want to spend a little time considering some introductory factors.

How we got the Ten Commandments

God told Abraham, who lived in Ur of the Chaldees, to pack his bags and move out. He didn't give him explicit directions; in fact He said, 'I'll show you where you are going when you get there.' Incredibly, Abraham from Ur of the Chaldees obeyed. When he arrived in what was subsequently to be known as the Promised Land, he discovered that it was no great shakes: Golda Meir, a former premier of Israel, remarked that God has a wonderful sense of humour: He gave His chosen people the Promised Land, and it's the only piece of real estate in the Middle East without oil!

This rather unpromising piece of real estate was handed over on a promise, by God, to Abraham. He said He would give him this land. He said that He would bless him, that He would make his progeny great; which was a startling prediction, seeing that he had no progeny yet. And He said that all the nations of the world would be blessed through this man Abraham.

This is what we call the Abrahamic Covenant. God was taking the initiative and making a covenant with Abraham that would have dramatically far-reaching effects, because in that covenant there was promise of blessing for all the nations of the world. If we go to the book of Revelation, we are reminded that ultimately around the throne of God will be people from every kindred and tongue and tribe and nation. This idea of an international church, made up of people of all generations, from all ethnic groups, is inherent in the covenant God made with Abraham.

The basis of this covenant was divine election and divine grace. There was nothing about Abraham that warranted its institution. It was a divine initiative; it was something that God, because He is God, freely chose to do. It is absolutely imperative that we understand that.

God also pointed out to Abraham that although this piece of real-estate was certainly going to belong to him and his progeny, it would not happen immediately, for two reasons. First, Abraham didn't have enough progeny to take over the land and populate it. Second, the people in the land at that time weren't bad enough to deserved to be kicked out. But God said, 'Just wait a little time.' Approximately 430 years later, something very dramatic happened. In the intervening years God had led His chosen people, the progeny of Abraham, into Egypt where they had suffered terribly under task-masters. But on the great day of Passover the Lord had wonderfully delivered the Children of Israel, and under Moses He had led them into the wilderness; and almost as soon as they got into the wilderness they had gone to Mount Sinai where the Lord spoke to them through His servant Moses; and there, among other things, He gave them the Ten Commandments.

The significance of the Ten Commandments

We must understand the significance of the order of events. *The Ten Commandments were given 430 years after the covenant of grace was established*. That might sound like an arcane piece of theological history, but it is fundamental to our understanding of the relationship between law and grace. The apostle Paul, as we shall see, made a very strong point of this when writing to the Galatians.

God had made a covenant of grace with Abraham and his progeny. Subsequently He gave the Ten Commandments, and other numerous laws that the Children of Israel were to observe.

The point is this: that they were going to observe the laws in the context of a life of faith based on grace.

Interestingly, the covenant which God made with Abraham, like other Old Testament covenants, is very similar to what are known as 'suzerainty' treaties. In ancient times each little town would have its own king; but there would be kings who aspired to become greater than that, and the way they went about it was to move into the area of the little kings and take it over. Eventually they would establish a suzerainty treaty, the basis of which was rather simple. The big king would look after all the concerns and the affairs of the little kings; and the little kings, out of incredible gratitude to the big king, would live a life of trusting obedience to him. That's the basic idea (very simplified) behind the structure of the covenant that you will find in the Old Testament.

Does this have any bearing for us? Oh yes, it does. Every one of us is like a little king or a little queen ruling over our own little domain. And the big king, Jesus, comes into our little kingdoms and says, 'I want to establish My kingdom here; and if, simply on the basis of loving obedience, you will submit to My kingship, then I promise to make available to you all that you need to reign in life.' Or, as the apostle Paul puts it quite specifically, to 'reign in life through the one man Christ Jesus' (Rom. 5:17). So we see this theme running not only through the Old Testament but also the New Testament; the Great King has taken the initiative to establish a covenant, a treaty of grace based on election, where He draws us into relation to Him and we are to live in loving obedience.

Thoughtful people would say, 'Well, how can I express my loving obedience?' God says, 'I'll give you ten ways.' We call them the Ten Commandments, or the Ten Words. Do they have significance for us today? Yes! But before we give such an emphatic, dogmatic answer we must allow for certain things. Some of you no doubt will be ready to quote Romans 6 at me:

> For sin shall not be your master, because you are not under law, but under grace. What then? Shall we sin because we are not under law but under grace? By no means! (Rom. 6:14–15)

You will often hear Christians say, 'We don't need to worry about the Ten Commandments. We're not under law, we're under grace.' When they do, simply reply, 'Granted. Now turn over to Romans 7.' In Romans 7:12 you will read, 'So then, the law is holy, and the commandment is holy, righteous and good.' Probably somebody will then quote Galatians back at you, particularly Galatians 2:15–16:

> We who are Jews by birth and not 'Gentile sinners' know that a man is not justified by observing the law, but by faith in Jesus Christ. So we, too, have put our faith in Christ Jesus that we may be justified by faith in Christ and not by observing the law, because by observing the law no-one will be justified.

To which, of course, you would legitimately respond by quoting Galatians 5:13–14:

> You, my brothers, were called to be free. But do not use your freedom to indulge the sinful nature; rather, serve one another in love. The entire law is summed up in a single command: 'Love your neighbour as yourself.'

A man once came to me after a sermon and said, 'Stuart, that was quite an interesting talk that you just gave; I thought I understood it—until you clarified it'! But it's very important that we wrestle with these apparently contradictory statements. On the one hand, Paul and the other apostles are apparently saying that the law has no bearing as far as the Christian is concerned, that there is nobody who is justified by keeping the works of the law, and that we are justified by grace through faith. On the other hand, those same apostles go out of their way to point out to us that the law is holy, righteous and good; and that we are to love, and that in loving there is a very real sense in which we fulfil the law.

So on the one hand they seem to be saying the law is not relevant to the Christian; and on the other, they seem to be saying that it is. Are we to fulfil the law—or are we *not* to fulfil the law? The answer to both questions is, of course, 'Yes'. But how?

First we must recognise the obvious fact that *we do not have to fulfil the law to deserve salvation*. No one is justified by the works of the law. However, while no one is justified by the works of the law, because the law of God is the reflection of His character and of His will those of us who are justified are being changed into His image. We are reflecting His character, we have a desire to fulfil His will and we do that in the power of the Spirit; not as a means of meriting justification, but as evidence that we have been justified by grace through faith, we live in accordance with the moral principles of the law.

What then is the significance, of the law for the believer? I would say that though it has no significance as a means of meriting or earning salvation, it has profound significance as a means of demonstrating that we have received salvation by grace through faith.

This should not be too difficult to understand, because in fact it's exactly how it worked in the Old Testament. That's why I took a few minutes to explain to you that before the law came, grace was established. The covenant of grace was that which God initiated and made available to men and women in His covenant people, so that by faith they might appropriate what grace offered and then, out of gratitude for grace, live a life of obedience.

What is the evidence of faith? Obedience. The apostle Paul is quite clear on this matter; writing to the Romans he actually talks about 'the obedience of faith' (cf 1:5). And in 1 John 2 we find clear evidence that the way we know that we are truly born of God is that we keep His commandments (cf 1 John 2:3–4). We cannot say that He is Lord and not do the things that He commands. And so we must establish the principle that no one is justified by the works of the law; but having been justified by grace through faith, the evidence of our gratitude for grace is seen in a life of obedience. The Ten Commandments demonstrate the character of God, they outline for us the will of God and they will become part and parcel of our life when the Holy Spirit writes them deeply on our hearts; and not only that, but gives us the desire and the ability to fulfil them—not as a means of salvation, but as evidence that we have been born again of the Spirit of God.

How do the Ten Commandments apply to us today?
Thirdly, how do the Ten Commandments apply today? Let me just give you five little pictures that may prove helpful to you.

The Ten Commandments, for the believer today, act like a *compass* that gives direction. They act like a *bridle* that gives restraint to a wayward horse. They act like a *thermometer* to measure devotion. They act like a *mirror* to show us reality. And they act like a *guardian* to bring us to Christ. Think of all these things, and you see the immense value of these Ten Commandments as far as the believer is concerned.

And now, after that rather long introduction, let us turn to the beginning of our Ten Commandments.

The First Commandment: Who is Number 1?

'I am the LORD your God, who brought you out of Egypt, out of the land of slavery' (5:6). The first thing mentioned in the suzerainty treaties was who the big king was and why he merited the loving obedience of his subjects. So the First Commandment begins with who God is and what He has done and why He deserves our trusting obedience. 'You shall have no other gods before me'—at the very beginning of the Ten Commandments, God makes it abundantly clear, on the basis of who He is and on the basis of what He has done, that He will brook no competition. He will accept no opposition, no gods before Him or besides Him.

The competition—'Other gods'
The Children of Israel, living in the land of the Canaanites, having come out of the land of the Egyptians, were well aware there was a plethora of gods available to them. So God makes it abundantly clear that they are a called and chosen people, a holy nation, a kingdom of priests, uniquely set apart to Him and for Him; and accordingly they must avoid any involvement with the gods of Egypt and Canaan and the surrounding countries and

must devote themselves unequivocally, unilaterally to the one Lord their God.

Wherever we go in the world, in whatever generation we have happen to have travelled, we will find that mankind has *a religious instinct*. There is something about human beings that makes them incorrigibly religious. Edmund Burke said, 'Man is by constitution a religious animal.' John Calvin said, 'A seed of religion is planted in all men.' The apostle Paul tells us that all human beings have a revelation in creation of the invisible God, and that everybody has to some extent a knowledge of Him (cf Rom. 1).

Paul quickly adds that though there are varying degrees of revelation and of understanding, human beings have one thing in common: they have all resisted the revelation made available to them. That is how he introduces his great epistle to the Romans. All human beings instinctively are religious. They know that they need to reach out to something beyond themselves; they recognise an innate insufficiency.

Atheism is a relatively recent invention and is never to be found in foxholes. When human beings find themselves under duress, if they haven't done so before they will instinctively reach out to something above and beyond themselves.

But mankind also has, besides an innate religious instinct, *a perverted ingenuity* which can make all kinds of things go wrong with mankind's innate religious instinct. A human being, having a feeling of inner inadequacy, might observe vast natural forces—storms, the tornadoes, hurricanes, thunder and the lightning and the force of the wind. And because he is overwhelmed and awe-struck by them he may well begin to think elemental forces are at work and will begin to treat them with awe and respect, seeking ways of placating them and getting these forces onto his side.

Or he may recognise that human survival imperatively demands keeping on the right side of nature, because nature has a wonderful cycle and that cycle goes on reproducing; and that he will note that he too has a reproductive capability. So he may join his own reproductive capabilities with the reproductive capabilities of nature and begin to devise not only religions that worship the elemental forces and seek to placate them, but also religious structures that involve all kinds of reproductive (sexual) activity, in order to get in tune with all the reproductive forces of nature. And—guess what?—because of his innate religious instinct and perverted ingenuity, the net result is a plethora of gods.

The Lord our God, the one who speaks to the people of Israel, says, 'You will find, in the regions where I am going to place you, a wide variety of gods. They are no gods. You will find a wide variety of religions. They are false. I am the Lord your God, I only am the Lord your God. And you must learn to differentiate between what is good and right and true, and what by definition is wrong and unhealthy and fundamentally evil. You shall have no other gods but Me.'

The Commandment—'No other gods'
The relevance for ourselves should not escape us. There is a plethora of gods available to us. There is a wide variety of forces operative in our world today that demand our allegiance. We find them most attractive, we find what they offer most desirable, and if we are not very careful we can find ourselves being awe-struck by them, seeking to placate them, trying to derive benefit from them. If we are not careful, we can move away from the Lord our God.

In marked contrast, however, to this plethora of gods available to the chosen people in Egypt and in Canaan, God has taken the initiative and revealed Himself. He has given them a Commandment, a very straightforward one: 'You shall have no other gods before me.' But He doesn't simply wag His finger at His people. He takes the trouble to reveal Himself to them.

Notice three things about Him.

The Lord our God, the Lord is one   In English this is a somewhat ambiguous expression: either He is unique, or He is a unity of being—it can mean both at the same time. He is unique in that He transcends all the other gods to which they may have been exposed, but—unlike the pantheon of pagan gods who often opposed and contradicted each other, leading people into all kinds of confusion—'The Lord is one. He is a unity.'

Perhaps this also gives us hints of the Three-in-One, the glorious community of the Godhead. Yet there is no confusion, there is no conflict in Him. The Lord is one.

2. The Lord is God   You'll notice in your Bible that the word LORD is in capitals. This means that it is a translation of the mysterious name that God chose to give Himself, 'Yahweh', as opposed to the other name 'Lord' (with a capital L and the rest lowercase), which is a translation of the Hebrew word 'Adonai'. The significance of LORD, the significance of Yahweh, is that it is the name by which God chose to reveal the uniqueness of His character.

The name 'Yahweh' is related to the verb 'to be'. How does that help us? Well, look at it like this. When God spoke to Moses and Moses said, 'I don't know your name', do you remember how the Lord answered? 'I am who I am' (Exod. 3:14) That phrase is related to the verb 'to be', so when God speaks about being Yahweh, also related to the verb 'to be', He is saying, 'I am who I am, I will be what I will be.' He is saying He is entire and complete in Himself, He utterly transcends all things, He is not contingent, He is not dependant, He is wholly other, He is one in and of Himself and He is utterly complete. And words fail to describe the uniqueness of the Lord.

The Lord, this unique One who is one, is God. That is the one who deserves and desires and demands our unequivocal allegiance. That is the commandment that He gives to the people.

3. The Lord is gracious   In verse 6 He introduces Himself as the one who brought them out of Egypt, out of the land of slavery. It was sheer unadulterated grace. He provided a means whereby they could be liberated from that which dominated them, and they were introduced into the freedom that only He could give.

So we have a revelation of God here to the people of Israel. The Lord is one, the Lord is God, the Lord is gracious; and He alone is the one whom you shall worship.

But notice the reasons for this stricture laid upon the Children of Israel. There are two particular problems over which the Lord was concerned for His people.

Syncretism   God knew that when His people overthrew the towns of Canaan, they would find that every little town had its local deity. And He knew that if they did not destroy all that was contrary to Yahweh in those towns, particularly those local deities, they might introduce the worship of these local deities into their worship of Yahweh. That is called 'syncretism'.

He gave strict instructions that when they moved into the Promised Land they were not to marry into the families of the indigenous people. Why? Because He knew that when the wife came into the family, she would bring all her belongings with her, including some of the family gods. So they were not to mingle their worship of the one true God in any way with anything of the pagan culture.

There is a long history of church missions in Africa. You often hear people saying that the church is growing by tremendous leaps and bounds in sub-Saharan and Southern Africa. Many African people are coming to faith in Christ out of tribal ethnic backgrounds. When those people get sick, there are no hospitals available for many of them. But some have been studying their Bible and have found that God heals. So they go to their minister from the West and they say, 'We understand that God heals. We have no hospitals, would you make sure that God heals us?' But some missionaries aren't quite sure whether God does heal today, or if He does, how He does it; so sometimes the minister waffles. But no problem, so far as the Africans are concerned. Haven't they paid their dues to the witch-doctor anyway? And it is not uncommon in Africa to find the elders and the deacons of the churches—evangelical churches—heading straight for the witch-doctor when they get sick. And how can that be?

Do I need to spell out the application? Is it possible that those who worship the one true God, the Three-in-One, might—out of carelessness and casualness about the culture that surrounds us, in which we live—be introducing into our worship of the Lord that which is contrary to Him? The answer is: Of course it's possible.

This is a monumental problem for the Christian today. On one hand we can spend all our time guarding against any hint of syncretism. On the other hand, we might be so concerned about reaching a post-Christian culture that we recognise we are going to have to do *some* things that relate to it; that if we insist on sticking with our traditional methods, we might manoeuvre ourselves into total, abject irrelevance. I wish I could solve the dilemma for you, but I can't; so I'll simply move on.

Sensualism   The second reason for this strict instruction is the need to avoid sensualism. I have already hinted at the very real possibility that the Children of Israel might become involved with some of the naturalistic religious principles of Canaan, where the people had developed all kinds of religious practices which included all kinds of gross sexual immorality. And the Lord knows that if He is going to call the people to Himself, one of the weak areas of their lives is the potency of their sexual drives. Nothing has changed. As worshippers of the one true God we need to be constantly on our guards against any hint of syncretism and any temptation to sensualism in our sexuality.

The Lord commands, 'Have nothing to do with those things that would even begin to lead you into that direction.' That is why He gives them such a straightforward command.

The choice—'Choose you this day'

Do you remember what Joshua said at the end of his life to the people of Israel after they had moved into the Promised Land?

> Now fear the LORD and serve him with all faithfulness. Throw away the gods your forefathers worshipped beyond the River and in Egypt, and serve the LORD. But if serving the LORD seems undesirable to you, then choose for yourselves this day whom you will serve, whether the gods your forefathers served beyond the River, or the gods of the Amorites, in whose land you are living. But as for me and my household, we will serve the LORD. (Josh. 24:14–15)

It was very straightforward. Remember Elijah and the prophets of Baal on Mount Carmel: how they built their altars and held that great contest to find out who was the true God? Elijah challenged them: 'How long will you waver between two opinions? If the LORD is God, follow him; but if Baal is God, follow him' (1 Kings 18:21)

You can't have it both ways. 'You shall have no other gods besides me.'

2: Deuteronomy 5:8–10

We come now to the Second Commandment. Let me just remind you that it is of the greatest importance that we should understand the context of the Ten Commandments as being within the covenant of grace. There are those who still struggle with the idea that you keep the Ten Commandments in order to deserve salvation, or with the idea that a person is justified by the works of the law. But that was never the case with Israel, and it never has been the case since. The covenant with Israel was a covenant of grace that was appropriated by faith and manifested by the obedience of faith. They were not obedient in order to deserve salvation, but in order to demonstrate their gratitude for having received salvation by grace.

It is the same in Christianity. 'It is by grace you have been saved, through faith—and this not from yourselves, it is the gift of God—not by works, so that no-one can boast' (Eph. 2:8–9). But in close proximity is Ephesians 2:10—'For we are God's workmanship, created in Christ Jesus to do good works.' Not 'by', but 'to do', good works. The covenant of grace is to be appropriated by faith and faith demonstrated by active obedience. That always was the principle; it still is; it always will be. If we can grasp that and underline it, we'll have no difficulty in seeing the relevance of the moral law of God, the Ten Commandments. We won't think of the Ten Commandments as being the means by which we warrant or merit salvation, but we *will* see the Ten Commandments as ways in which we live in obedience and demonstrate a love for the Lord and gratitude for His covenant of grace.

The Second Commandment: Making God in our image

Thomas Watson, the old seventeenth-century preacher, observed that in the First Commandment worshipping a false god is forbidden; in the Second Commandment, worshipping the true God in a false manner is forbidden.

The Second Commandment warns, 'Be very, very careful that in your attempts to worship the true God you do not use false methods.' Part of the human problem is that we are very material entities. We have material bodies, we live in a material world, we are relating constantly to material dimensions of human. But we are also spiritual entities. So if we are to live in the fullness of our humanity, we are called to live our spirituality in a material environment—the only environment in which we can live it. The Lord Jesus, you remember, in prayer to the Father immediately prior to leaving His disciples, said three specific things which are a constant challenge to me. He said, 'I am going to leave you in the world'; 'You are not of the world'; but 'You are sent to the world' (cf John 17).

I suggest that the whole of our human existence is intended to be lived out in the tension of those three things. God in His wisdom has chosen that we, spiritual-material entities, should live spiritually in a material world. But we are not to be of it. There is to be something distinctive about us. But we are not to be so distinctive by being separated that we are utterly irrelevant to it, for we are left in it, not of it, but sent to it. And the major challenge for us is, holding those three in tension, to find spiritual fulfilment in a physical, material environment.

If that is so, material beings having spiritual aspirations can only operate on the basis of human imagination, unless they are in tune with divine revelation. That's all we've got to work on. So if human beings are *not* in tune with divine revelation, they are in some sense locked in to human imagination. And human imagination will start working from the material to the spiritual, instead of drawing from the spiritual and applying it to the material. When that is the best that human beings can do, guess what happens? They formulate spiritual entities in material ways. And that's how idolatry comes about.

So we are utterly dependant upon divine revelation, if we are to know truth. Truth does not come from human speculation and human imagination. It comes from divine revelation. And now God is granting to His covenant people vast revelations of Himself, and He is saying, 'Draw from these revelations and respond to them and translate your spiritual experience through revelation in the material world.' The problem was, the Israelites were surrounded by people who didn't have the revelation, so they were operating on speculation and imagination; they were fundamentally material and they were into all kinds of idolatry.

In this context, let me ask you: is it possible that we, living Christianly in our present-day culture, could be out of tune with divine revelation and more in tune with human speculation and human imagination? Tell me, is it? Of course it is. If so, what happens? 'All kinds of idolatry.' So there is a profound application of this passage.

The denunciations of idolatry
Now let me identify for you three things here regarding idolatry.

1. Scripture denounces idolatry   What did God have to say on the subject? Number one, 'Do not represent the creator by anything created.' It's probably the ultimate insult. Paul makes a strong point of this in Romans 1, where he says that every human being has, in the creation, some revelation of the creator; but people have not only resisted it, they have chosen to represent the creator by created things. As a result they have come under the wrath of God. Notice the tense: 'The wrath of God is being revealed from heaven' (Rom. 1:18). There is a sense in which the wrath of God will be revealed eschatologically, in the future, but there is a sense too in which the wrath of God is being revealed at the present time against people who resist revelation and choose to substitute the created for the creator.

Paul proceeds to answer the question, 'How is the wrath of God being revealed at the present time?' He has revealed His judgement against these attitudes by giving people over to the consequences of their own choices. In His sovereignty He gives us the freedom to choose, but He does not give us the freedom to choose the consequences of our choosing.

You might ask, 'To what has He given us over?' Paul goes on to answer this question too. Romans 1 tells us: confusion about deity, which leads inevitably to confusion about humanity, which leads inevitably to confusion about sexuality.

Let me ask you: Is there any confusion about deity in Britain today? Is there any confusion about humanity in Britain today? Is there any confusion about sexuality in Britain today? You are seeing the judgement of God in Britain on every hand. It is actually taking place at this time.

God says that you are not to render to anything that which belongs to God, for God is a jealous God. Does that bother you? Is God a green-eyed monster? Perhaps a better word is 'zealous-y'. He is zealous, He is enthusiastic for, He is energetic towards, He is totally committed with phenomenal vigour, to His own integrity; and He will not allow people to mess with it. God has demonstrated this by saying that if people persist in substituting the created for the Creator, if they insist on preferring speculation and imagination to revelation, He will allow people to move off into their error. And the tragedy is this that when that happens, error filters down to the next generation, and the next, and the next. We see it on every hand. God allows His judgement to come.

But please notice that the God who allows the consequences of human sin to filter down into generation after generation that hate Him, also brings His great grace to thousands who love Him. The grace of God will always overwhelm the wrath of God when people respond to it.

So God denounces idolatry; He absolutely, categorically denies human beings the right to represent the Creator by the created. He will under no circumstances allow anything to be given the place reserved exclusively for God. We must not miscalculate God's reaction to this. He is zealous for His own righteousness, and He will allow judgement to come and percolate to other people if they continue to resist Him—but He will always reach out in grace and mercy to those who respond to Him.

2. The prophets and apostles were called to denounce idolatry   In Isaiah 46:1–8, with considerable irony, Isaiah portrays a people who manufacture idols which have to be carried from place to place and cannot move at all on their own. In marked contrast, God made all people; He carries them; and He doesn't stay where He's put. So why in the world would anybody be more interested in an idol than in the one true God?

If they hadn't had any revelation you might say, 'You can hardly blame them.' But Romans 1 tells us that they have had a degree of revelation. But the tragedy of the people of Israel is, they have had the revelation of the one true God and they are now slipping into idolatry.

Is there a lesson for us here? Oh yes. It is perfectly possible for those who have a vast amount of revelation of God in Christ to slip carelessly, callously, into all kinds of activities and attitudes that show quite clearly that they are forgetting the revelation available to them. They are simply preferring the created to the creator.

And what did the apostles have to say in denouncing idolatry? The apostle Paul addressed some trenchant remarks to the Corinthian church, to the effect that idolatry must be studiously avoided, that we must recognise that though in one sense there's absolutely nothing in the idol, behind it there can be demonic forces. So we must always be on our guard, so that we do not slip into worshipping the created instead of submitting to the Creator. And one of the most trenchant things Paul says is that greed is idolatry.

Now we've really come down to application, for when we begin to desire to accumulate or acquire for ourselves what has been created, and those things become more significant to us than the Creator—then we have slipped into idolatry.

3. Scripture gives us many clues concerning the dangers of idolatry   Idolatry makes means into ends. The original purpose of making idols (the material things) was that it would help the people to work from the material which they understood, to the spiritual which they didn't understand. The idols were a means to an end. Some of my Roman Catholic friends at home tell me, 'Protestants accuse us of idolatry. They say we make idols of the Virgin and of the statues. We don't. These things are simply material things to elevate our thoughts to the spiritual ends.' I'm sure in some instances that's exactly what they are. But you know as well as I do that in other instances the idols have become the end in themselves. And that is the danger of idolatry.

Is it possible that in our lives we can have some things that are intended to be a means towards the end of worship, but have in reality become an end in themselves?

Let me give you an example: music. Would you say that music is a legitimate part of worship, a means to an end? But is it possible that we can become so wrapped up in our own approaches to music that it becomes an end in itself and we forget to worship? We have every kind of worship in our church. We go from Bach to Rock. And people occasionally express opinions on the matter. We have a group in our church called Blue Grace. They play hand-clapping, foot-stomping stuff. It's kind of wild—and it's good, once or twice in a while. One of our senior ushers used to walk out whenever they played. He said to me the other day, 'Stuart, I've been reading my Bible. It says there, "All our righteousnesses are as filthy rags." I am so self-righteous when it comes to music. God is saying to me, "All your self-righteousness in this matter too is filthy rags." Stuart, I've got to stop being critical and I've got to start worshipping.'

We can make an idol out of music, either worshipping it or resenting it so much that we forget that it's simply a means to an end. A lady in her seventies in the church once came to me and said, 'Stuart, I was irritated by the music on Sunday morning. I was composing a letter to you in my mind. A little voice seemed to say to me, "I thought you came for corporate worship?" I said I did. The little voice said, "No you didn't, you came for personal preference. The place for personal preference is at home, and the corporate worship is here. Now look around the body of believers and see if they are worshipping." So I did, reluctantly, and to my horror I discovered that they were.' She continued, 'I want you to know something. In the future, when there's a style of music I don't appreciate, I won't sit there fuming. I'll look around and say, "Oh, look at those people worshipping!" And I'll thank God that these people are praising Him.'

Here's another problem. *Idolatry substitutes things for the person*, when this dumb idol, piece of wood, rock, or piece of metal that is intended to point people to the one true invisible God becomes in and of itself a substitute for the person Himself. Is it possible in our experience for that sort of thing to happen?

When at twenty-nine I left the business world and began in full-time ministry I was rather excited. But soon afterwards I contracted a throat infection so serious there was a real possibility I would not be able to talk again, let alone preach. So far as I know it was the first and only time in my life that I succumbed to depression. I was paralysed by it, until one day, a thought occurred to me that was just like the Lord speaking. 'Stuart, what is it you love? Preaching about Me, or Me about whom you preach?' Honesty forced me to admit, 'I love preaching about You more than I love You about whom I preach.' And He said, 'That's exactly why you are where you are right now. If you ever get around to the position of being prepared to love the One about whom you preach more than preaching about the One you profess to love, I'll give you your voice back.'

You can make an idol out of preaching, out of your Christian service, out of your commitment, because idolatry is not only substituting means for ends, it is also substituting things for the person. Idolatry places imagination above revelation. Is there a possibility of that in our world today? Oh yes. We have a lot of unchurched people turning up at our church (we love it; I ask those who disapprove of all those uncommitted people turning up, whether they'd rather the people had stayed in bed where they would run no risk of becoming committed . . .). Not infrequently one of these uncommitted people will come to me after I've preached on the character of God, and say, 'Stuart, I couldn't believe in a God like that.' Usually they believe in a God of love and of grace and of mercy; they're not too excited about a God who's also righteous, a God of judgement, a God who is a jealous God, a God of fierce, pure and holy anger. In other words, they are making an idol out of imagination; they reject revelation. There's no question, I believe, but that if we are not extremely careful, it is all too easy to decide what aspects of the divine revelation we will accept, and where we prefer to substitute our human imagination for what God has told us He really is.

Here's another danger. *Idolatry imposes limits on divine transcendence.* God transcends all things in the sense that He is utterly other, utterly different, utterly beyond anything that we know. 'To whom will you compare me?' (Isa. 40:25, 46:5), says the Lord. And therein lies one of our problems with idolatry. Idolatry takes transcendence and squashes it down into human limitations.

Solomon struggled with this. He was almost apologetic in his prayer of dedication for his magnificent temple: 'Oh Lord, the heaven of heavens cannot contain You, what in the world can this house do?' (cf 1 Ki. 8:27) Of course the answer is that this house couldn't contain Him, magnificent temple though it was. The problem with idolatry is that if we are not careful we can circumscribe the transcendence of God and cut Him down to our own ideas, squash Him into our traditions and limit Him to what we regard as acceptable. When we have got Him into our box of traditions and determined the limits of what is acceptable as far as God is concerned, we've finished up with *our* god. We have limited transcendence.

One of the great dangers in the contemporary church is that some want to push the limits out and explore other areas of spirituality, of speculation and imagination, and some are nervous and are all the time trying to hold back, saying that they are going to 'stand firm on the revelation'.

Most of here today would come into the category of conservative evangelicals. Is there a possibility that conservative evangelicals are so concerned about Christians wanting to push out onto the extremes and possibly fall into error, that we have so circumscribed the transcendence of God that we have limited Him to our puny traditions and locked Him into what we will find acceptable? We wouldn't dare to actually say so—but we have decided what God can do with our permission, and what He's not allowed to do. If we are not careful, we may find ourselves engaging in idolatry.

The Third Commandment: What's in a name?—Introduction

I want to end by briefly introducing the next Commandment to you.

Verse 11: 'You shall not misuse the name of the LORD your God, for the LORD will not hold anyone guiltless who misuses his name.' The old version used to say, 'Thou shalt not take the name of the Lord thy God in vain.' Many people think this just means you shouldn't swear. And certainly swearing and oaths are inappropriate for the Christian, in that sense of misusing the name of the Lord. But there is much more to misusing the name of the Lord than swearing.

Juliet, in Shakespeare's *Romeo and Juliet*, asked 'What's in a name?' The implication was, 'Nothing.' But she was wrong. There's an awful lot in a name.

Just before I was born my father was reading a book called *In the Heart of Savagedom*. It was about some intrepid missionaries in what was then the Belgian Congo. He was utterly taken with these people. The author of the book was a single lady from Dublin, whose surname was Stuart-Watt. He said to my mother, 'If the baby's a boy, his name is Stuart.' As soon as I was able to understand, he told me, because he wanted me to understand that my name had nothing to do with Scotland but everything to do with his hope that I would grow up to have a ministry.

I once preached in a church in Belfast and dutifully shook hands with everybody afterwards. As the church was emptying a tiny wizened old lady approached. We got into conversation. She said, 'Will you come and be our pastor?'

I said, 'You have a pastor.'

'I know, but he's no good. If you'll come we'll get rid of him.'

I asked why she wanted a change. She said, 'They don't like me in this church.'

'I'm sure they love you!'

'No they don't. They don't like me because I bring prostitutes to church. They sit there looking all stuffy down at me and I bring in these beautiful prostitutes. Now I think you'd like those prostitutes. And I think they would like you. So you come and be our pastor.' She reinforced each point with a rather disconcerting poke with her umbrella.

Eventually I tried to extricate myself. 'I really must go. But you didn't tell me your name.'

And she said, 'My name is Eva Stuart-Watt.'

It was the sister of Miss Stuart-Watt who had co-written the book. There she was in her nineties, still poking preachers with her umbrella, still bringing prostitutes to church, still with vision and drive and enthusiasm.

I tell you, I'm grateful for my name, because every time I hear it I am reminded of my father; and every time I am reminded of my father I am reminded of a faithful man, and I am reminded that he was committed to ministry and he wanted me committed to ministry.

Is there anything in a name? Oh yes. But that's just my name. What about THE Name? Come tomorrow and hear the next exciting instalment.

3: Deuteronomy 5:11–15

The Ten Commandments were given 430 years after God had taken a divine initiative and established a covenant of grace. We are not justified by the works of the law, we are justified by grace through faith. We do not keep the law in order that we might be justified, but having been justified by grace and drawn into a covenant relationship with God, we then respond to His grace by a life of obedience. That is the fundamental principle which allows us to recognise the place of the Ten Commandments in the life of those who have been saved by grace. There is a place for the obedient keeping of the moral law, not as a means of justification, but as evidence that we have been redeemed by grace.

The Ten Commandments are divided into two sections; they were written on two tablets. Some have suggested, though it can only be speculation, that the first four were on one tablet and the other six on the other. But the first four are certainly helpful in showing us how realistically we love God and the last six are helpful in showing us how practically we love our neighbour as ourselves.

Yesterday we began to look at the Third Commandment.

What's in a name?—the question in a general sense
We saw that, contrary to the opinion of Shakespeare's Juliet, there is a great deal in a name, especially when you see how names are used in Scripture.

Names can be intended to convey reputation   God took great exception to the people of Babel who wanted to build a tower. The reason was that they were going to build it to demonstrate their independence of God—and 'to make a name for themselves'; they were interested in developing a reputation for themselves independent of God. The book of Proverbs reminds us that 'a good name is more to be desired than riches'. And in a familiar passage of Paul's letter to the Philippians, he talks about the self-humbling of the Lord Jesus and the exaltation of the humbled Lord Jesus. The pinnacle of the exaltation is that He is given a name which is above every name, so that at the name of Jesus, every knee should bow. Why? Because of His reputation as the great triumphant, once-crucified, risen and ever-living Lord.

Names are often used in Scripture to describe character   Sometimes people are given new names. Jacob was given a new name, Israel. Simon son of John was given the name Peter. Joseph the Cypriot was given the name Barnabas. And there was profound significance in these names, because they conveyed something of the character of these people. I said yesterday that the reason that I treasure the name that I was given is that it was given to me by my parents, who had a great desire that the character of the person who originally bore that name might in some way be projected in my experience.

Names in Scripture are used for identity   A person's name is a means of identifying them among all the millions of people on the face of God's earth.

When I was serving in the Marines I attended the Naval Gunnery School in Gosport, Hampshire. The first hour of the course was spent learning the name of the commanding officer. The reason was that he had a habit of coming up to recruits, tapping them on the shoulder with his swagger-stick and asking, 'Who am I?' We had to spring to attention, salute smartly, and reply, 'You, Sir, are Major-General Sir William Leach-Porter, KCB, DSO, MC.' You can see that I learned it well! One young man from South Yorkshire was so overcome by the sudden appearance of the CO resplendent in his magnificent uniform, medals all over the place and scrambled eggs all over his hat, that he replied, 'Oh aye, now just a minute, thou's Leach-Porter.' He was hurried away and we never saw him again . . . But I assure you that 'Major-General Sir William Leach-Porter, KCB, DSO, MC' is a superb way of identifying one particular man, who for some reason did not seem to know who he was but had nevertheless risen to the rank of Major-General.

Names are an introduction to intimacy   If you want to share intimacy with a person and you are British, you may choose to give them the freedom to call you by your first name. If you don't want to be intimate with them you will expect them to call you Mr or Mrs for the next twenty-five years at least. If you become really intimate you may allow them to share your pet name, your nickname. This is one of the great transitions that has to take place when a Britisher goes to America. The first week I was in America, three total strangers knocked on the door and greeted me with the words, 'Hi, Stu.' I didn't know what to do with them so I did what the British do when they don't know what to do; I invited them in for a cup of tea. They were all insurance salesmen.

What's in a name?—the question as relating to the Name
We know that there is profound significance in the name of the Lord. If you've never done so before, get hold of a concordance some time and dig out all the different names that God has chosen as a means of revealing His character and revealing His reputation. And you will revel in the discovery, for you will find that you not only have the opportunity of knowing who He is, discovering what He has done and identifying what He promises, but you'll find in a study of His names that He invites you into intimacy with Himself. What's in a name? A vast amount of potential experience.

God chose to reveal Himself by His name, and did so progressively. To Abraham He revealed Himself as El Shaddai, the almighty God. But He reserved the revelation of Himself as Yahweh until Moses. It was as if He were adding one further revelation of His character, reputation, purposes and promises on top of another. God makes Himself knowable, He gives us the possibility of being introduced to Him.

There's something so stiff and so formal about people who need to be introduced, who can't move into a relationship, like the old story of the two Englishmen, stranded on a desert island and rescued years later: they hadn't spoken to each other the whole time, because they hadn't been introduced . . . But God has not only revealed His character, reputation and purposes—He's invited us into an intimacy with Him, introducing Himself to us and saying, 'Call me Father. Call me Saviour, call me Friend,' and He goes down the list of His names. What's in a name? There's so much in a name.

Misusing the Name

The question for us now is this. If we recognise all that is involved in the revelation of God's reputation, character and purposes, and the possibility of being introduced to Him in His name and invited into intimacy with Him, is it possible that we can abuse this? The answer is clearly yes; we can. We can abuse our knowledge of Him. We can abuse the opportunity of being introduced to Him. We can abuse the incredible privilege of intimacy with Him—or, if you like, we can misuse the name; we can take the name of the Lord in vain. That clearly involves swearing, it clearly involves oaths and curses. But to limit it to that is, I think, to miss the point.

Let me suggest one or two practical ways in which we can be and should be on our guard in this respect.

We can talk a lot about the name of the Lord, but in actual fact be more interested in making a name for ourselves   In church life it's possible to masquerade as somebody who is in ministry 'for the Lord's sake'; but if we are honest we may have to admit that we are more concerned about making a name for ourselves in ministry. The symptoms are that we so often get hurt in ministry. We feel we aren't getting the recognition that we deserve, aren't being appreciated as we might be, that people aren't really grateful and do not remunerate us as they should; and we find that although we say that 'we are not in this for me, we are in it for Him', we begin to discover that our reaction to the circumstances of ministry is such that it becomes abundantly clear that there's an awful lot of us in it. There's an awful lot of my reputation at stake. We're eager to make a name for ourselves. Watch it! Because, you see, the Lord will not share His glory with another person.

We can pray outrageous prayers 'in the name of Jesus'   One of the nice things about being a grandparent is hearing your grandchildren pray. Often they pray the most outrageous things, and end their prayers with the words, 'for Jesus sake.' Of course we excuse that in children. But it's alarming when you go to a church prayer meeting and hear adults praying outrageous things, purportedly in the name of Jesus. Sometimes our prayers are utterly self-centred and self-interested; but we tack on the end, 'for Jesus' sake', so purportedly it's His name, it's His glory, it's His concern, it's His kingdom I'm interested in. But if I know my own wicked heart, it isn't. I'm praying in His name for my personal benefit.

Do you see the challenge to us in the early part of the Ten Commandments? The Lord is saying, 'If you love me, I'm going to be Number One. You're going to have no other gods beside Me. Nobody's going to make any idols. And you're not going to abuse My name, because you are going to understand who I am and you're going to relate rightly to Me.'

It is perfectly possible for us to call on the name of the Lord without really committing ourselves to His lordship   In weddings at our church, I ask the couple to say to each other these words: 'I give thee this ring as a token of the covenant made between us this day, and as a pledge of our mutual love, in the name of the Father and of the Son and of the Holy Spirit.' That's quite a statement. The ring is just a token and a symbol, but it is a token and a symbol of a commitment, a covenant and a promise made in the name of the Father, the Son and the Holy Spirit. When you look at what happens to some marriages, you have the awful feeling that the name of the Lord was invoked without a commitment to the Lord in the context of marriage. Sisters and brothers, be very careful. It is possible to take the name of the Lord in vain.

It is possible to use His name in ways that are intended to convey great significance but don't necessarily do so When I took up my pastorate just over twenty-five years ago, there was one group in the congregation that just about filled one pew. I thought they were absolutely wonderful; they used to pray while I was preaching. When I said something, down would go their heads in prayer. Months later I discovered what they were praying about. They were praying, 'Oh Lord, get this man out of this pulpit.' They told some friends of mine, who challenged them without my knowing, that the Lord had told them to stay and pray me out of the pulpit.

I tried to talk to those people, but everything they said was prefaced with, 'The Lord told us.' It puts you in a very awkward position when you are talking to people who have that hot line for which you don't have the number for.

But they are long since gone and I am still there. So either the Lord didn't tell them, or they are living in rank disobedience. You get my point? 'The Lord told us to stay here and pray this man out of the pulpit.' Be very, very, very careful how you use the name of the Lord. It's a very important matter. The Lord is to be revered and honoured. And one way of doing it is by having that deep regard and respect for His name.

The Fourth Commandment: This is the day

The Fourth Commandment (verses 12–15) is a long one. Let me point out to you first of all some things that we need to understand about biblical teaching on the Sabbath. The first thing to remember is that the Sabbath is not introduced for the first time in Scripture in the Ten Commandments. We know for a fact that God rested on the Sabbath day, and we know from the teaching in the Ten Commandments in Exodus and in Deuteronomy that there is a very definite link between God's rest in creation on the seventh day, and the Sabbath day.

The second thing to remember is that after the Children of Israel were brought out of Egypt and were wandering in the desert they were fed with manna. The people were required to collect the manna every morning. On the seventh day it didn't come fresh from the heavenly bakery, but on the day before it came in double quantities. They were not allowed to collect on the seventh day. Why? Because they had already been introduced to the idea of Sabbath.

The meaning of the Sabbath

Sabbath means 'day of rest'. It is a creation ordinance, a fundamental principle of creation. In exactly the same way that the physical creation has physical laws, so the spiritual, relational and the sociological creation has, built into it, divine creation laws. An example from the very beginning of creation is that God made human beings male and female: 'For this reason a man will leave his father and mother and be united to his wife, and they will become one flesh' (Gen. 2:24) This is a creation ordinance for the well-being of society—a sociological principle. The law of thermodynamics is a physical principle; the law of the Sabbath is a creational ordinance. He underlined it in their experience in the wilderness and then He instituted it as a command in the Ten Commandments. This is what He said: Men and women will work six days a week (that gives us pause for thought regarding our five-day week immediately). And they will take one day a week off, the Sabbath.

It became even more complicated. As you read further in the history of Israel, you discover that every seventh year there was a year off, as far as the land was concerned: and every seven-times-seven, on the fiftieth year, there was a year of jubilee. It was a built-in principle, one designed to show that for human well-being, there has to be a rhythm. We talk about biorhythms—this is divinely ordained rhythm. It's a rhythm of work and rest. It's a rhythm of worship and recreation. Human beings' well-being is related to working and worshipping and resting and recreating. It was divinely ordained. And it was something that human beings are required to maintain. Why?

Scripture explains that there three good reasons for keeping the Sabbath.

God rested at the time of creation   He was modelling something for humanity; that it was right and proper for men and women to work, but that they must not become workaholics, so absorbed with their work and with making money, with getting on in the world and with keeping up with the Joneses and overtaking them, that they do not build time for worship into the rhythm of their lives. It's the easiest mistake in the world to make. The busier we become, the more successful we become, the easier it is for the rhythm to be disrupted. If God found it necessary to model the necessity of worship for us in the context of work, who are we to suggest anything different?

Notice that Deuteronomy provides a different explanation from the one that we have in Exodus. Exodus says that we should observe the Sabbath day because God did so at the time of creation. In Deuteronomy, we are told we should observe the Sabbath day because,

God delivered the Children of Israel who were slaves   This doesn't seem to have any significance at all, until we read it in its context: that not only you are to have the right rhythm of work, worship, rest and recreation, but you are responsible for seeing that those under your authority have the freedom to do so as well. 'Because,' God says, 'remember that while you may be in authority over others, at one time you were a slave; and when you were slaves you were abused. But I delivered you from your abuse; so—make sure that you are not abusing yourselves by not having the right rhythm of work and worship, but make sure too that you are not imposing on other people a limitation on their ability and opportunity to work and their freedom to worship.'

God said that the Sabbath was to be a sign between Himself and His chosen people   In chapter 31 we are given a third reason to observe the Sabbath. It is evidence of a covenant that God has made with the people. He chose them to be a holy nation, a people set apart for Himself. And if they were going to be holy and set apart, it meant among other things that they were going to be unique and distinctive in the midst of the nations.

So we develop a principle of the Sabbath in order to have a

right rhythm of worship, work, rest and recreation; in order not to abuse other people's freedoms; and because we are a covenant people who are different. The Lord speaks a Commandment to Moses: 'I am your God; you shall have no other; you will not have idols and worship them; you will not misuse My name; and you will honour Me in the rhythm of your lives.'

When you put all those together, it's easy to see how covenant people are distinctive people. They live among other people who are not the Lord's people; and as they—according to His principles—demonstrate, in obedience, out of gratitude to Him, that they love Him intensely and immensely, so their life-styles point unerringly to Him.

The desecration of the Sabbath

One of the things that happened very quickly in the history of Israel was the desecration of the Sabbath.

You can read about it in Nehemiah 13. It was to be expected that the people who had come out of captivity and had gone back to rebuild Jerusalem, who were going to get the Temple rebuilt, would really be aware what it meant to be the covenant people. One would expect that they, of all people, would be concerned to honour the law of Moses. But in fact that was not the case. They were showing marked disinterest in worship and utter disobedience in life-style.

But there was an entirely different problem in the days of the Lord Jesus, for He discovered that certain of the people were so into Sabbath-keeping that they had laid law upon law upon law, so that people were weighed down with all the rabbinical instruction. I think they started out with a deep desire to do it properly. They didn't want to break the law inadvertently, so they asked for interpretations. They knew that they should not engage in sowing, but then a rabbi noticed seeds sticking to the clothes of some people walking through grass one Sabbath. Then the seeds fell off. 'You're sowing!' said the rabbi, and henceforth it was forbidden to walk through grass on the Sabbath.'

They found all kinds of ways of making their own rules. They were totally absorbed in nit-picking, minute externals, and deep in their hearts they had lost their love for the Lord.

So you have here two entirely different problems. On the one hand, you've got some who lapsed into legalism; and on the other side, you've got the people who've lapsed in licentiousness, they've become libertines. And it was ever thus.

When we look at how we approach the Sabbath today, we will see some people who have no commitment to work, to worship, to rest and to recreation. There's no rhythm, there's no structure, there's no balance to their lives. They just drift. They're just casual, they do whatever they like. There's no sense of ordering their lives before the Lord. And then there are other people whose lives are weighed down with innumerable man-made laws. And not only that, they judge each other's internal spirituality by the way in which they adhere or don't adhere to their particular system of man-made laws.

So the question before us is this. If we are to honour the Lord by a life of loving obedience, we keep His commandments. But keeping His commandments doesn't just mean we learn the Ten Commandments by rote and say 'I live by them.' What it *does* means is that we take the time to get into their meaning and relevance, so that we live lives of loving obedience in the glorious liberty of the sons of God.

4: Deuteronomy 5:16–18

We are going to look this morning at the Fifth, Sixth and Seventh Commandments.

The Ten Commandments were given 430 years after God had established a covenant of grace, so that people might respond to the covenant of grace by loving God with all their hearts and minds and strengths, and their neighbours as themselves. God gives them ten ways to do it; the first four showing how to love God with all their heart; the last six, how to love their neighbours as themselves. These are moral teachings, to be obeyed because they come from the heart of God. They are appropriate for Christians. They are not a means of salvation, but are a means of demonstrating our loving gratitude in terms of trusting, loving obedience.

But the Ten Commandments are also applicable to those who are not believers. This is something we have not yet stressed, because Keswick is primarily a meeting of those who are members of the covenant of grace and believers in our Lord Jesus Christ. But the function of the Ten Commandments for the unbeliever is to show us the exceeding sinfulness of sin and lead us to repentance so that we might cast ourselves in utter dependence upon the grace of God, manifested in Christ who died and rose again for us.

I often remember a story told in the Cumbrian mining town where I grew up, in the days when huge ugly slagheaps dominated the town. A lady living in a cottage near one of the slagheaps hung her washing out, and was delighted to see how magnificently clean it looked against the black slag background.

She forgot to bring it in overnight. During the night it snowed, and the slagheaps were covered with pristine white virgin snow. She went out, and her laundry seemed yellowed and grubby. In fact, it hadn't changed at all. It was just that she was seeing it contrasted with a different background.

Our world is full of people who are perfectly satisfied with the lives that they live because they are comparing themselves with the wrong background. Human beings are prone to look for somebody worse than themselves, to measure themselves against them, and because they are clearly the better, to assume that they're all right. Our laundry looks wonderful against the black slagheap, but if we hold it up against the law of God, God's moral standards, we will see that it hasn't changed at all, our sinfulness was sordid and tawdry all the time. And that will lead us to repentance.

So if you are not a believer and are not a member of the covenant of grace, this is relevant to you too. As we look at what it means to honour the Lord and to love our neighbours as ourselves, we fall humbly before the Lord and we say, 'I haven't done that, and I need His grace and His forgiveness.' And that, of course, is available to us.

The Fifth Commandment: Life in the family

Honouring our father and mother presupposes that we know who they are, and know them so well that we appreciate their significance; and also that we are living in a relationship with them that allows us to express our appreciation, respect and admiration of them. All that is wrapped up in that simple little expression, 'Honour your father and mother.' It speaks of that fundamental relational block that God has ordained for the well-being of humanity, called the family. It is a statement concerning the way that we live in family and conduct ourselves in family, in the relationships with those who brought us to birth.

Scripture of course has much to say on the subject of family and in a variety of ways. The tribes were vast families; the tribes were divided into clans, containing large numbers of people; and within the clans were what we would now call 'extended families'. There's probably greater emphasis in the Bible on the extended family than on what we would now call the 'nuclear family'—mum and dad, 2.4 children, a dog and a television.

The changing family

Few think in terms of tribes or clans today, and most of us would have difficulty in identifying our extended family. Some of us do not even live in a traditional nuclear family at all, because there has been dramatic fragmentation in that area of modern life.

Some futurists have suggested that before long it will be practically impossible for a person to honour their father and mother, because they'll have no idea who they are. It's possible that in the future a human being can be created by an egg donated by one person, impregnated by a sperm donated by another person, conceived and nurtured in the foetus of a surrogate mother; who then had two parents who took the child only to then divorce and remarry. It may sounds ludicrous, but I assure you that that is the present trend. There has been a dramatic change in the fundamental ideal of family, which is integral to the idea of honouring father and mother. And of course that means that we need to be very clear about what the Scriptures teach about the family.

The family in biblical times

Notice that in this Commandment we are told to, 'Honour your father and your mother, as the LORD your God has commanded you, so that you may live long and that it may go well with you in the land the LORD your God is giving you.' One obvious advantage of this structure of the family so far as the Children of Israel was concerned, was that it was going to enhance the possibility of *economic survival* for them in the land where they were going to live.

Secondly, the family is ordained for *emotional stability*—'so that . . . it may go well with you'. God has ordained that children should be brought into a relationship with a father and mother so that they can mature, and develop an appropriate psychological, sociological and spiritual integration in their personhood. We learn these sociological, spiritual and psychological health factors in the context of a living, caring family unit.

The Scriptures also make it clear that the family is necessary to provide *an educational structure* in which people can be given the chance to grow up in the nurture and admonition of the Lord. Had we time we could look into Deuteronomy 6, where we find that God is giving instructions about the children of those to whom He is speaking, and their children's children. He roots what He is saying to these people in what He gave to their fathers. So there was the generation He was talking to, there was the preceding generation, there was the succeeding generation, and the generation that would succeed them. And the point of it all is that God is saying, 'My word must be maintained, My word must be taught in all these areas.'

I submit to you, things have not changed; the structure of family as divinely ordained still assists people in economic survival, emotional stability and a healthy educational structure. That is why it is important.

The family today and tomorrow   Some of the dramatic changes have perhaps been helpful and some have clearly been detrimental.

We have already noted a dramatic change from extended family to nuclear family. But there is a dramatic move away from the traditional nuclear family at the present time. There has also been a great move away from the sense of a hierarchy to individuality, so that people now feel perfectly free to do their own thing without any sense of accountability to those to whom one would traditionally have expected them to be accountable.

And there has been a great move away from stability to mobility. A man brought up in the Italian district of New York once told me, 'I never got into trouble. I wasn't a saint, not at all. We just had a big Italian family. In the whole neighbourhood where I lived, I never could go anywhere without an uncle or and aunt seeing me.'

There was community, care, nurture, oversight, accountability. And you know as I do that most of those things have now gone. It's not surprising that we find many people growing up psychologically damaged, spiritually inept and sociologically dangerous. It is so, because we have departed from the principles that God ordained for families.

Now what does the Christian do about this?

Christian attitudes to parents   The Christian recognises that the father, the mother and the children; the parents of the father and mother, the children of the children and the children of the children's children are all part of a whole, and that God has ordained this networking of relationships so that there can be a deep involvement of each in the lives of others, a caring and a nurturing. If we move away from that, we do so to our extreme detriment.

Now, let's be very simple and practical. If we are committed to our family, what does it mean to honour our fathers? What does it mean to recognise the work of a father? What does it mean to honour your mother? What does it mean to recognise the value of a mother? Ask yourself, 'How can I express to my father my deep appreciation of his worth to me? And how can I reach out and express to my mother my deep appreciation for that in which she invested in my life? Have I ever done so?'

In America the theory of victimisation is popular. It argues that nothing anybody does is their fault. They have absolutely no responsibility for it. All that they are and all that they have done is because what their fathers and mothers did to them. And the reason their father and mother did it to them is because of what *their* fathers and mothers did to them. It's wonderful! You freely admit that you've done things that you shouldn't, that you aren't what you should be—but it's not your fault! So no guilt attaches, and so no shame is necessary, and so no repentance is appropriate. So you just get on living your messed-up life saying, 'It was their fault.'

God had a trenchant word to say about this through the prophet Ezekiel. In his day there was a proverb: 'The fathers eat sour grapes, and the children's teeth are set on edge' (Ezek. 18:2). Did you know, God banned that proverb? There's an element of truth in it, of course, as we have seen: 'I, the Lord your God, am a jealous God, punishing the children for the sin of the fathers to the third and fourth generation of those who hate me, but showing love to a thousand [generations] of those who love me and keep my commandments' (Exod. 20:5–6). But the point is that men and women had to accept that while what they did was indeed affected by what their fathers and mothers and forebears did before them, they were still responsible.

This means that I must look realistically at what I am, what I've done; that I take the trouble to find out what my father and mother did that contributed to that, and accept the fact that they were partially responsible. I must accept that that they have developed propensities in my life, but that I am responsible for the way I utilise those propensities. Though it will allow me to see the things that my father and mother didn't do right, it will allow me to accept responsibility for what I've done. And at the same time, I am prepared not merely to refrain from blaming them but to accept the fact that there were many things they did right.

That was the title of a lovely book published some time ago in America: *What They Did Right*. In it several well-known believers spoke very positively and helpfully about what their parents did right. May I suggest that you sit down and write (if you haven't done so already) a short essay entitled 'What My Parents Did Right'. If they're still alive, send it to them.

The Sixth Commandment: The sanctity of human life

The NIV translates this, 'You shall not murder.' Older versions read 'Thou shalt not kill.' The NIV reading is much more helpful. A great many Hebrew words in the Old Testament and other Hebrew writings are translated 'kill'. Also the Bible would be contradicting itself if all killing were banned in the Ten Commandments; later in Scripture we find God giving instructions that certain categories of people are to be killed. We must differentiate carefully.

The significance of this Commandment
The Old Testament law does not impose a blanket prohibition on all killing. It does distinguish between totally illegitimate killing and other kinds which in certain circumstances are not only appropriate but are even necessary.

For example, a clear distinction is made between murder and manslaughter. Provision is made for what were known as the 'cities of refuge', to which you could go if you accidentally killed somebody by what today we would call manslaughter. If you got there before the relatives of the dead person got to you, then they couldn't touch you. On the other hand, God gave clear instructions to the people when they arrived at the Promised Land to utterly destroy the people in some of the Canaanite cities.

So what is it that is prohibited in the old words, 'Thou shalt not kill'? *The prohibition is against all acts of premeditated killing based on vengeance, malice and anger.* Now, the rationale for this needs to be clearly understood. Scripture teaches us that humanity is made in the image of God, and makes this fundamental statement: 'Whoever sheds the blood of man, by man shall his blood be shed; for in the image of God has God made man' (Gen. 9:6). If somebody in a premeditated way, out of malice and anger and vengeance, takes another person's life, the Old Testament principle was that that person's life is forfeit because that person had done despite to what was made in the image of God.

Human beings are part of the animal kingdom. We know that because when we experiment by putting pigs hearts into human bodies, they work. Many of the surgical advances that we enjoy were first tested on dogs, because a dog's physical structure resembles our own in some ways. We are part of the animal kingdom—but obviously different from it. Why? Because we have the ability for conceptual thought, we have the ability to be part of the divine creative purpose, we have moral sensitivity, we have been given the ability to communicate with God, to receive His revelation, to appreciate it and to express that appreciation in worship—all to show the uniqueness of our humanity. There's nothing like us, we are something else, we are utterly unique, and we have an eternal dimension.

Some people, of course, believe that we are just slightly higher than the apes. The Scripture has a much more appropriate view of us. It says we are just a little lower than the angels—and that we need to recognise our uniqueness. And that's the point; if we can begin to understand the uniqueness of our humanity, we can begin to understand what a dreadful thing it is to destroy that which in the divine economy is so utterly unique; it is totally abhorrent to God. To destroy what is uniquely created in the divine image is to challenge the divine intent in making that person. To murder is to abrogate divine authority and to take into our hands that which belongs only to God. 'Vengeance is mine,' says the Lord. To end human life is to despise the divine evaluation of that human being.

The relevance of this Commandment

You may be tempted to say, 'Well, I wasn't planning on murdering anybody so this isn't terribly relevant.' I'm sure you weren't. However, some profound problems confront the Christian in today's culture; abortion, euthanasia, capital punishment, warfare, suicide—and we do need to be thinking about what is going on here. Let us look at two of them.

The abortion issue   A believer's attitude be to abortion depends on what you believe the unborn child to be. If you believe that the unborn child is simply part of the mother's body and that the mother has inalienable rights to her own body and rights to privacy; and if you believe that the government has absolutely no jurisdiction inside the woman's body and over her internal organs, then you will probably ask, 'How dare the government intrude on a woman's rights?'

On the other hand you may believe that that foetus, that unborn child, is a human being in process; that human life begins at conception; that the Bible teaches the possibility that the child in the womb has some sense of divine activity (for unborn children in the Bible were known to leap with joy when someone came into their presence, and we are told that in our mother's womb we are fearfully and wonderfully made). And if you believe that the unborn child is that which is uniquely created in the divine image, then it will be utterly abhorrent to you even to begin to think in terms of destroying that unborn child.

So if we are concerned with the sanctity of human life, obviously we will take a very definite stand against using abortion as a means of birth control—a convenient, premeditated way of getting rid of an inconvenience.

Some say that it's slightly different when the unborn child is the result of incest or rape. Equally Godly people will take different positions on this, because we must be concerned not only with the sanctity of the unborn life, but also with the well-being of the born life of the mother of the unborn child. There are profound dilemmas in this area. There's no place for slogan-eering. Once, having condemned euthanasia and abortion on demand when speaking to our church, I was rebuked by one of my young associates afterwards. He asked me, 'What are you *for*? You spent all that time telling people how opposed you are to abortion on demand, but you didn't spend thirty seconds telling us what you are for. According to the counselling I do, by the law of averages there must have been among all those people you preached to this morning ten and twelve women contemplating abortion for all kinds of reasons. And all you did was condemn them. What are you *for*?'

I replied, 'I'm not sure I understand your question.'

He said, 'Well, let me help you. Wouldn't it have been helpful if you tried to be sensitive to what goes on inside a woman's mind if she finds herself with what is euphemistically called an "unwanted pregnancy"? Wouldn't it have been helpful if you'd not only shown sensitivity but compassion to her? And wouldn't it have been wonderful if you could have called the church to begin to open their homes and families to women in such a situation, to embrace them and love them and care for them and help them to bring the child to term and lead them into the possibility of considering adoption rather than abortion?'

He was right. And there's obviously much more we could say on the subject, but haven't time to do so here.

The euthanasia issue A generation ago Francis Schaeffer pointed out to the church that if abortion became accepted, it would be only a matter of time before euthanasia became normative. It was a prophetic word.

'Euthanasia' comes from two Greek words: *eu*, meaning 'good' or 'well', and *thanatos* meaning 'death'. It means 'good dying', or 'good death'. The idea behind euthanasia is that people have the inalienable right to die when they are ready, to avoid unnecessary suffering, to determine when they will cease to be a financial drain on their families; to decide when they are going to die.

There's a tremendous struggle going on in the United States over legalising euthanasia. They call it 'physician-assisted suicide'. This is a great irony. The Hippocratic Oath clearly bans euthanasia. Doctors are not in the business of helping people to die but of helping people to live. So it's imperative that we remind people that their responsibility is not to assume that they have the right to govern their own living and their own dying, but to recognise that God in His goodness has brought them into the world until He determines it is time to take them out of it. It is not our right, it's His responsibility.

Having said that, we need to be very careful to distinguish between prolonging life artificially and not allowing people to die when God apparently wants them to. There is a difference.

Those are two of several areas in which the Sixth Commandment is relevant today. Let me now take you back to where we started. The Lord Jesus made it abundantly clear that He wasn't only concerned with acts of murder, but also with the roots from which much taking of life comes. He was talking about heart-attitudes, about anger, about ungovernable rage, about deep resentment and anger that is not properly handled. And He said that it was from these heart-attitudes that the entire fruit of this kind of killing comes. In the great hyperbolic way in which He made these profound statements, the Lord Jesus in effect said that the one is like the other.

Of course there's a difference between saying 'I'll kill you if you do that,' and actually doing it. But there is a clear link between fundamentally wrong inner motivations. We might sit here rather smugly this morning and say, 'Well I've never murdered anybody, I've never had or performed an abortion. The only fight I've been involved in was a Just War according to Aquinas' definition. As far as I'm concerned, I'm in the clear on this one.' I have a very simple question for you. Have you got an anger problem? Have you got a resentment problem? Have you got a malice problem? Have you got a rage problem? Because, you see, that is the root from which the others come.

The Seventh Commandment: Preserving the sanctity of marriage

The prophets, the apostles and the teaching of Christ Himself make it clear that adultery has always been a problem. Adultery is illicit (because extra-marital) sexual activity. The Bible teaches that from the beginning of creation, God created them male and female, and for this reason a man will leave his father and mother and cleave to his wife, and the two shall become one flesh (cf Gen. 1). The 'one flesh' has, among other things, sexual connotations.

Sexual activity outside the bonds of that marriage is prohibited by God. Some people today would say, 'Why? I have an appetite for food, so I eat; I get thirsty, so I drink. I have a sex drive, so I do what comes naturally. If God has given me these appetites, these drives, why in the world should I not satisfy them in any way that I find appropriate?'

Let me give you a few reasons.

Why adultery is prohibited
The first reason is that *adultery defies God*. When God says, 'Don't do it,' and I say, 'Oh yes I will,' I shake my face in the fist of God.

Second, *adultery destroys families*. A member of a family may have sexual relations with somebody other than their marital partner and may quite possibly derive some degree of satisfaction and fulfilment in doing so; but while they are doing that, they are damaging their spouse and they are doing desperate damage to their children, and, if the partner in adultery is married, to their spouse and children. And I promise you, there's a very high probability that it will lead to the disintegration of two families. And I also promise you that if the family disintegrates it will leave deep scars on the children which they will take into their own marriages and simply perpetuate the scarring. Our daughter Judy did her PhD research at the University of New York and her dissertation, that went to hundreds and hundreds of pages, is on the subject of the impact of divorce on adolescent development. And it's bad, bad news.

Third, *adultery defiles marriage.* Marriage is a covenant based on commitment. When a person engages in adultery they defile the covenant, they break the promise, they show themselves to be untrustworthy and faithless. It has a defiling impact upon all those involved.

Fourth, *adultery denies love.* Love is committed to the well being of the person, regardless of their condition or their reaction. When a person engages in adultery they are saying to their spouse, to the other partner and to the spouse of the other partner, 'I am totally disinterested in this concept of love as a commitment to the well being of the other person. I could not care less about your well being. All I'm interested in is my satisfaction.' That attitude must never ever be confused with love.

Fifth, *adultery derides faithfulness.* Read Proverbs 2. Read Malachi 2. You will see some dramatic pictures of what really happens when a person breaks covenant and breaks faith.

Sixth, *adultery degrades people.* There's a high possibility of physical damage, there is no question that it causes emotional scarring, and there is profound communal impact and a deep spiritual implication.

The causes of adultery
What are the causes of adultery?

First, *standards that have ceased to be regarded as absolutes.* Nowadays we say, 'If it's right for me it's right, if it's wrong for you it's wrong.' That moral ambivalence causes deep uncertainty in many people, particularly young people. The second cause is *lust.* The third is *unfulfilled desires and unsatisfactory marriages.* Much of the counselling we do in the church in America is about sexuality. We find that when men get into an adulterous liaison, it is usually because of lust. When women do, it usually has to do with loneliness. They do it for the care, the compassion, the concern, the fellowship, the encouragement that they are not getting from their husbands. Take heed! The fourth cause is *undisciplined lifestyle*; the fifth, *unconfessed sin*. Adultery doesn't start with the sex organs. It starts with the organ between your ears. That's why the Lord Jesus said that it is in the heart that adultery takes place.

The cure for adultery

You may say, 'I've never committed adultery, I've never killed anybody and I don't speak badly of my parents.' Let me ask you something. Have you ever been resentful? Have you ever been lustful? Have you ever imagined in your heart the possibilities of moving out from the restrictions of the commitments you have made? Have you ever thought, 'If only I'd had the chance, I wonder what it would have been like?' Have you ever found yourself dealing with ungovernable rage or anger, or deep resentment? Have you ever found yourself maliciously ripping somebody apart? I have. And whenever I do that, I don't love my neighbour as myself. Whenever I do that, I'm not living in the depth of covenant relationship with my God that I should. Do you know what's necessary? Repentance and confession and cleansing.

But just supposing I'm talking to somebody here this morning who has had an abortion. Let me assure you, there's forgiveness for that. Am I talking here to somebody who has killed, and nobody knows? There's forgiveness for that. Let me tell you, whatever it is that you have done in thought or word or deed that contravenes the moral standards of the holy God, there's forgiveness for that.

It calls for coming to terms with it, deeply repenting of it, openly confessing it and willingly receiving that which God alone can give you because Christ died for you.

5: Deuteronomy 5:19–21

Introduction

There's a great debate going on in America at the moment, and I suspect in Britain as well, about values. I believe it's one of the most productive areas for Christian witness today. There are widely divergent lifestyles in the cultures of our Western democracies. Behind every lifestyle is a system of values. And while it is relatively easy to criticise or applaud a lifestyle, if our response is to be appropriate it is imperative that we understand its underlying system of values.

By 'system of values' is meant a collection of those beliefs that we hold so tenaciously that they determine our behaviour. Translated into action, they produce a lifestyle. If we are going to live appropriately as Christians in a pluralist society where people have the freedom to develop different lifestyles, we need to know how to relate to and communicate with our contemporaries; which means that we need to take the trouble to understand their lifestyles and value-systems. Much more than that, we must understand from whence they derive that value-system.

Sources of values

There are three basic sources of a system of values.

The assumption that everybody is free to do what they like
This is the principle of the autonomous self: 'I am my own person, I do my own thing, what I do with my life is my business

and none of yours, I am responsible and accountable to nobody; I just do my own thing.' Think of your neighbours. Think of your colleagues at work. Can you understand their lifestyle? Do you understand their system of values, and do you understand that many of them are operating on the basis of the autonomous self? It doesn't take much thinking to realise that no society can survive if it is made up of people who are exclusively committed to the self. Fortunately, there are some people who say there's a second way of determining your system of values.

The recognition that everybody is part of society John Donne said, 'No man is an island.' And many people accept that they are no islands, but they would like to live like archipelagos, or groups of islands. Recognising that nobody is an island, we tend to decide our system of values according to what society (not the self, for that's unrealistic) decides is appropriate. This is the way in democracies; certain issues come up, the people vote and the majority decides what is 'right'. It becomes law. That is how we operate. But this itself poses all kinds of problems, for society is made up of a lot of selfs, each deriving a system of values from the autonomy of their own desires.

This was very well illustrated some time ago by the comment of a United States Supreme Court justice talking about a pornography case. 'We're having a very grave problem with this matter of pornography. We all know it when we see it, but we don't know how to define it.' In the end the Supreme Court ruled that pornography is 'that which offends'—listen carefully!—'local community standards'. Note the subtlety of that. What would not raise an eyebrow in Times Square New York would cause a heart attack in rural Illinois. That which people wouldn't think twice about in Soho would give people a fit in Cheltenham.

The acceptance that we are created in the image of God

The third source of values accepts that we are not autonomous; that we are more than members of society; that we are each a unique person created in the image of God, who comes from

Him, lives through Him, exists for Him and is accountable unto Him; and that He is the one who determines what is good and right and true. In the revelation of His character and His purposes, I discover my system of values, and I translate that into the application of His system of values in my own life through obedience to His word and dependence on His indwelling Spirit.

There will be little similarity between the lifestyle of somebody who operates on the basis of the autonomous self and somebody who operates under the benevolent dictatorship of the sovereign Lord. And obviously, if we simply operate on the basis of what is acceptable to the majority, there's a very high possibility that the society of which we are part will determine that something is acceptable which is totally unacceptable to the sovereign Lord. And herein lies the challenge for the Christian.

It is imperative that Christians should understand that they are coming from God, that they are living for God and through God and are accountable unto God; and that it is in the revelation of His character and His purposes that they discover what is good and right and true, and that in the power of the Holy Spirit, in obedience to the Word, they begin to generate a lifestyle in the midst of all the conflict and confusion of our Western civilisation. This gives us a glorious opportunity to live differently, distinctively, winsomely, powerfully, attractively; because deep down, people recognise that those values which are reflections of the character and purpose of God are the noble, grand things.

But it also gives us a great opportunity to understand why people are thinking differently and to engage them in discussion at that point of the issue of values.

One of the great practical values of studying the Ten Commandments is that such study gives us a firmer under-girding for our own system of values. It gives us what will generate in us a distinctively different lifestyle, but it also gives us something with which we can begin to address the conflicting confusing lifestyles of those amongst whom we live.

The Eighth Commandment: Handling resources responsibly

In Commandments Five to Ten we are learning how to love our neighbour as ourselves. If we are living in love towards other people, we are primarily concerned with their well being. That's a fundamental condition of agapé love: to be primarily concerned with their well being, regardless of their condition or reaction. And if that is your motivation and your desire there is no way you can steal from a person, or lie to or about the person, or begrudge what that person has and desire to have it for yourself. But given our sinful fallen selves, I think we will discover that we have a marked propensity to break these commandments, perhaps in ways we have not considered.

'You shall not steal.' Scripture teaches that it is possible for us to steal from human beings, and it is also possible for us to steal from God.

Stealing from people
How can we steal from another human being? The obvious answer that springs to mind is,

Deprivation of property There's currently a tremendous emphasis on rights in our culture at the present time, much of it appropriate and much singularly inappropriate. But the Bible, not least in the Ten Commandments, says very little about rights and a great deal about responsibilities Yet the interesting thing is that to the extent that we fulfil this second section of the Commandments, the other person's implied rights are met. 'Thou shalt not steal' implies the right to have property. 'Thou shalt not bear false witness' implies the right to be treated honestly. And so we could continue.

Scripture does emphasise the right to property. If you read on in the book of Deuteronomy you find that though a person could become utterly destitute, even being forced to surrender their family and finally themselves into slavery, and though a person could acquire such heavy debts that their property had to be handed over to secure the debt, there were very definite rules prevented people being forced to the point where their basic necessities were taken from them. You couldn't take their mill-stone, if you took their cloak as collateral security you had to give it back each night, and so on.

The apostle Paul, writing to Timothy, reminds us that if we have housing, food and clothing, we should be content (cf 1 Tim. 6:8). The implication is that it is perfectly legitimate to own property that is necessary for human existence.

Deprivation of liberty   God has given people freedom to function under His control. We are created in His image to serve Him, and are given the privilege of functioning according to His dictates in the community of people in which He has placed us. But some wicked people who will deprive a person of that liberty. A young married missionary called Mark Rich went from our church in Milwaukee to serve in Panama. He and two others have been a prisoner of guerrillas there for over two years. It is a wicked thing; they are stealing from those young men what is legitimately theirs—their liberty.

Deprivation of dignity   There is a dignity to human beings created in the image of God, and if we decide that we have the freedom to demean somebody or to diminish their reputation, we are stealing from them the dignity that is inherently theirs.

There were riots in Ephesus when Paul was there, provoked by the shop steward of the union of silver smiths. He got very upset because Paul was ruining their business. One of his complaints to the authorities was that the great goddess Diana was being robbed of her dignity by what Paul was doing.

It is possible to demean somebody and thereby rob them of their dignity.

Deprivation of opportunity   God has granted to us as human beings great opportunities to achieve things for His glory and for the well being of other people. But some people are able to deprive others of opportunities to exercise what God has insisted is their total freedom to do certain things.

I am a pastor in a church, one of a group of elders. We are responsible for major decisions that will affect the lives of thousands of people. If we make wrong decisions, we may well be depriving those people of opportunities that God has given to them. It is a fearful thing to be leader in the Christian church.

I was reading the Parable of the Talents when the thought occurred to me: if the master was singularly unimpressed with somebody who buried his own talents, what would his attitude be to those who buried other people's talents? And then I realised that it was possible for me to have a profound influence on what my wife and daughter were given the freedom to do; I realised that if I wasn't very careful I might one day have to stand before God and hear Him ask me, 'Why did you deprive your wife and your daughter of the opportunity to exercise gifts that I clearly had given to them?' That's a word for men in the church.

I fully understand that there are many issues involved in the issue of women's role in the church. But one of the major issues, and I fully recognise this, is that a leader in the church it's possible for me to deprive women of the opportunities that God has clearly given to them.

Stealing from God
We can steal from people, but we can also steal from God.

Robbing God of His due   In the book of Malachi we are reminded that God instituted a system where people could demonstrate their gratitude to Him for all that He had given to them, because, as God had made it clear, it was He who gave people the ability to get wealth. So He instituted the tithe system. There was a ten percent tithe, then every three years another tithe and on top of that there were to be offerings—sin offerings and thank offerings. (Some people talk about tithing and they have a fit when they think of ten percent. But that was just where they started!) Now, in Malachi God has a complaint against His people. He asks, 'Will a man rob God?' And the answer is, 'He sure will, if he gets the chance.' They wouldn't admit it. 'Wherein have we robbed you?' He said, 'In tithes and offerings' (cf Mal. 1).

'Thou shalt not steal' means 'Thou shalt not deprive another person of that which is legitimately his or hers—and thou shalt not keep for thyself that which is his.'

As a small boy in my father's grocery store I watched him counting the money at the end of the day. I noticed him putting it in two boxes and asked him why. He replied, 'Because that's God's box and this is ours.' He was giving me a simple initiation into the principle of first fruits. Not giving to God only what you can spare; giving to God, off the top, the first fruits as an expression of gratitude to Him. And he went on to tell me, as he put the money into the two boxes, 'We never ever touch what isn't ours.'

You know, one of the great scandals of the Christian church is that it is almost always broke. It's not because it doesn't have resources. It's because there are too many sticky fingers hanging onto the divinely imparted resources. I worked out that if our congregation all became unemployed and went on welfare and tithed that to the church, we would have so much money that we wouldn't know what to do with it. It was one of the least popular talks I ever gave to our congregation.

Can a man rob God? Yes, of course he can. How in the world can we handle this tendency to want to deprive others for our own benefit and deprive God to meet our own selfish needs? What can we do about it? I think one of the things we can do is to decide whether we believe what we believe. Can a man rob God? Do we believe that he can? Yes. Do we know how we can rob a person or rob God? Well, think it through; if we know how we can do it, then we must ask ourselves the question, 'Am I doing it?' And if we are doing it, then we must say, 'Well—what do we need to do to rectify this situation?'

One way is to develop a generous spirit towards other people, with the desire to affirm them, to encourage them, to give them opportunities even when it means stepping back from some of the opportunities yourself. C. S. Lewis says that one of the great problems as far as our giving is concerned is that we never know how much is appropriate. Then he suggests perhaps the only appropriate way to give is to give until we feel we are giving too much. There's a lovely occasion in the Old Testament when the Children of Israel were given the opportunity to give, and in the end the leaders had to say, 'Please, no more, no more' (Gen. 36:6–7). They had to be restrained from giving! As far as I know, it's the only time in church history that it's happened.

If you have been stealing, repentance means putting it right, and restitution is imperative. W. P. Nicholson once held an evangelistic campaign in Belfast. Many shipyard workers attended. He preached to them about repentance and restitution. They began to take back to the shipyards what they had stolen from work. In the end, the shipyard owners had to appeal for the restitution to stop. There was no room to store all that had been returned.

What a wonderful thing! It's called revival.

The Ninth Commandment: Speaking the truth

Our judicial system requires us to tell 'the truth, the whole truth, and nothing but the truth.'

Were you inflicted with television coverage of the O. J. Simpson trial over here? Many who watched came to the conclusion, rightly or wrongly, that people who had sworn that they would tell 'the truth, the whole truth and nothing but the truth' were lying, and that many of the lawyers involved in the trial were less interested in finding out the truth than in winning for their client.

In America there has been a great erosion of confidence in the legal system. If there is one area in which you would expect truth-telling and a desire to deal with the truth, surely it is there. If it has begun to disintegrate there, is it any surprise that truth-telling is at a premium in the rest of society? But God specifically prohibits lying. He is committed to truth. You will remember that Jesus made it abundantly clear that the Devil was a liar from the beginning, and it is under his influence that people become strangers to the truth.

Why do people lie? There are at least three reasons.

One is that we get into *defensive lying*. We know the uncomfortable truth about ourselves and that if it comes out we will be in trouble one way or another. So if we don't want to be in trouble we will cover up the truth. We will lie, we will deceive, in order to defend ourselves against the just consequences of our wrongful action. This is a very common, ongoing kind of lie.

Then there is *destructive lying*: the kind of lie designed to ruin another person. I know that what I say about that person isn't true, but I don't like that person, I'm jealous of them, they are doing better than I am. Somehow or other I know I can't beat them by the truth. I can't beat them on a level playing field, so I'm going to have to tilt it in my favour. I will insinuate into the situation things that are just not true about that person.

The third reason for lying is *deceptive lying*: lying not out of genuine error, but saying palpable untruths, intending to deceive, in order to gain an advantage.

So I must recognise that God is committed to truth and that the evil one is the author of lies, committed to error and deception. I must recognise that it is quite possible that I in my own fallenness have the ability and the tendency to defend my position by the use of untruth, by being willing to deceive another person to gain the advantage; willing to insinuate what is palpably untrue into a situation, so that I can defeat what I cannot compete with.

There's a delightful balance in Scripture on this matter. It says that we should be committed to 'speak the truth in love' (Ephesians 4:15).

Notice the balance! Sometimes in our commitment to 'truth' we will present something that may well be true, but in an aggressive, offensive way. Perhaps the motivation when we 'tell the truth' is to hurt and to damage. And there is the other extreme; sometimes we are so committed to 'loving that person' that we will avoid telling them the truth. One of the great tragedies in many of our churches is that so often we have on one hand truth-tellers who are unloving, and on the other hand lovers who no longer tell the truth. We have issues that need to be addressed and others that need to be not addressed, in the name of love.

The balance is very straightforward. Here is a rule of thumb: give credit where it is due and you will be qualified to give criticism where it's necessary. But don't you dare think that you somehow have the inalienable right to criticise somebody where you deem it necessary, if you have not taken the trouble to give that person the credit where it was due. Why should anybody accept criticism from you, if you have never invested positively in their lives? But if you have, is there not all the more likelihood that they will be prepared to accept criticism from you because they know the positive influence you have—criticism that is necessary, speaking truth in love?

The Tenth Commandment: Forbidden fruit

It's very interesting that this final Commandment finds its way into the Ten Commandments at all. All the others have to do with actions; this one has to do with attitudes. But all actions have their roots in attitudes. So if we are ever going to address the actions, we need to get to the root causes of attitudes: attitudes towards God, attitudes towards others, attitudes towards ourselves. Have we come to terms with who God really is? Do we want, above everything else, for God to be God? Have we come to the point of a realistic evaluation of what we are— uniquely created, eternally significance, deeply loved, wonderfully gifted, profoundly significant in the economy of God . . . but totally depraved?

That's right: 'totally depraved'.

The doctrine of total depravity is one that I believe needs to be proclaimed loudly and clearly so that it can be understood. The most helpful definition that I am aware of comes from Dr J. I. Packer: 'Total depravity does not mean that man is at every point as bad as he could be, but rather that man is at no point as good as he should be.' Brilliant! In other words, my attitude towards God is, 'God, You are my creator, You are my redeemer, You are the lover of my soul, You are the securer of my eternal destiny, You are the one who gives me the ability to make wealth, You are the one in whose hand my breath is, You are the one who makes it possible to be, to exist, and to survive, You are the one alone in whom I find my significance and my purpose; and You love me and I submit myself joyfully to You and I live in dependence upon You and my overwhelming desire is that You might be honoured in my life and that Your kingdom might be established in my life.'

And getting the right attitude about God also means saying, 'I have come to a realistic appraisal of the gifts You have given me, and of my obvious flaws. I understand myself warts and all, and I recognise what I can do and can't do, what I am and what I'm not; and I want to present to You that which is salvageable. I want You to take it and use it. I want to present to You that which is only worthy of destruction, and I want you to work on it so that I might be conformed increasingly into Your image. And I need to have a different attitude to people; Paul said that we now no longer view people from a purely human point of view, and I have to admit to You that I need a major attitudinal switch, for I'm afraid I have a terrible tendency to view people from a purely human point of view. I avoid or nurture relationships according to whether or not I decide I dislike or like the people concerned and often for what I get out of the relationship.'

When there is a major change in our attitude to God and in my attitude to myself, there is a major change in my attitude to other people. I begin to look at them through the spectacles of God. And I begin to see them as creatures of inestimable value, utterly fallen, potentially redeemable, eternally significant. I say, 'God, I am so sorry I've made such a mess of my life. But I'm glad you still love me. I ask You to forgive me and I would like to embark in newness and freshness of life, on this principle—in utter dependence upon Your enduring Spirit, I commit myself to live in obedience to Your word. And I believe that the result will be an increasing development of my life in a manner that will honour You, bring great blessing wherever I go and enrich me beyond my wildest dreams.'

THE ADDRESSES

'The Awesome Presence and the Guilty Conscience'

by Dr Steve Brady

Isaiah 6

> Where is the blessedness I knew
> When first I saw the Lord?
> Where is the soul-refreshing view
> Of Jesus and His word?
> (*William Cowper*)

In 1976 I came to Keswick with my wife for Holiday Week. The previous year I had entered marriage and the ministry within three weeks of each other; now I was tired and jaded after twelve months of ministry. Of the thousands of words we heard that week, one sentence stuck especially in my mind. It came from the lips of someone who is a good friend of many of us, Alec Motyer. This is what he said: 'You've lost your vision of God.' And, amidst all the hurly-burly of major changes in my life, amidst all the demands of being a young Christian minister, I realised afresh why I was at Keswick. I needed a soul-refreshing view of Jesus and his word. And I thank God for that week, which helped to re-orientate and re-calibrate me.

If there's one great problem with the church of Jesus in our land and as we see her in Western Europe, and with many of us as individual Christians, it is that we have lost our vision of God. Cowper's words are the plaintive cry of many hearts. I wonder whether, this evening, that's your problem too; that you've lost your vision of God. Indeed, much of our society is marked increasingly by a sense of the absence of the presence of God. It marks our increasingly-felt moral and spiritual vacuum.

So we turn to that wonderful passage in Isaiah 6 to help us regain our vision of God. I am going to limit myself to four points which I hope will be simple and memorable. I suggest that this passage causes us to look up to God, to look in to ourselves, to look to the provision of mercy and atonement He makes, and then to look out as our response to the grace of God.

Look up

'In the year that King Uzziah died, I saw the Lord . . .' Isaiah had lived through some of the reign of Uzziah, who had reigned for fifty-two years on the throne of Judah. By and large it had been a good and benevolent reign; he had been on the whole a good king so far as kings of Israel and Judah went. Unfortunately he ended rather badly. In 2 Chronicles 26 we are told that he was greatly helped until he became powerful; verse 16 says that 'after Uzziah became powerful, his pride led to his downfall', for he intruded on the holy office of the priesthood and sought to offer burnt offerings and burn incense. As a result he became a leper until the day of his death. He is a salutary warning to us all, especially if we are getting on in years, because he started very well but finished rather badly.

A wise old Christian man prayed daily from his middle years, 'Lord, save me from becoming a wicked old man.' He knew his Bible. He knew the Solomons whose hearts had been turned from the Lord by their wives, and all the decisions they had made in the past. Uzziah finished badly. God save us from a wicked old age.

But Isaiah illustrates the principle that no one lives to him or herself, that our decisions have implications on others—especially if we are in positions of authority, and he was the king—and our influence can be profound. Though Uzziah was a fairly good king, he helped to leave a dreadful legacy to his nation. Go through the opening chapters of Isaiah and you'll see cruelty, idolatry, pagan superstition; you'll see some of the 'isms' that we face today. Materialism flourished in various parts and

God was left out of the picture. Hedonism ruled; pleasure, pleasure, pleasure, with very little thought for God. God was excluded from the picture. And there was moral crisis. Look at 5:20. 'Woe to those who call evil good and good evil.' Isn't that a commentary on Great Britain in the late twentieth century? Some of us can remember the time not long ago when, even in the back streets of Liverpool where I lived, little children were safe, front doors were left open and old folk were liked and respected. Today we live in a topsy-turvy world of moral and spiritual crisis. Isaiah summarises it all in 1:6: 'From the sole of your foot to the top of your head there is no soundness—only wounds and bruises and open sores, not cleansed or bandaged or soothed with oil.' This was a sick, evil society which nominally bore the name of God; the people were supposed to be God's people.

Into that picture, Isaiah comes. Uzziah, who had been the centre of a modicum of political stability in this heaving moral and spiritual mounting crisis, is now dead. 'In the year King Uzziah died'—a major prop of society has been taken away. A little bit of salt, albeit compromised salt, has been taken from the scene; and things are going to get worse. Perhaps you've come to Keswick this year and some major prop has been taken from your life, too. It may be a life partner, a close friend; maybe some financial security you were banking on for your old age. Maybe your health has failed, someone's let you down, some Uzziah has died for you. And you are wondering how you are going to make it through.

Well, God in His mercy at such times delights to come to His people. For God gives to Isaiah what every believer needs; a fresh vision of His being and of His ways, of His immensity, His power, His glory and His availability to their needs.

'In the year that King Uzziah died, I saw the Lord . . .' The Bible tells us plainly that 'no-one can see God and live' (cf Exod. 33:20), and John tells us in his prologue, 'no-one has ever seen God' (John 1:18). So is this a contradiction? No. It's just a reminder that the infinite God, who cannot be contained by anything or anyone, accommodates Himself to us. He shows us here a part of His nature, He shows us as it were the hinder part

of Himself. It is what the theologians call anthropomorphism;
Isaiah is explaining in visionary form something that is impressed upon his heart, spirit and mind as he sees the living
God. 'In the year that King Uzziah died, I saw by contrast,' he
says, 'the deathless God, the immortal king, the eternal king, the
eternal Lord—I saw the Lord.'

Do you notice how he saw Him? Sitting on a throne, as a mark
of His authority? Daniel 4:35 reminds us of Nebuchadnezzar's
lesson: 'He does as he pleases with the powers of heaven and the
peoples of the earth. No-one can hold back his hand or say to
him: "What have you done?"' The God who is encountered
here by Isaiah, the God of all authority, is high and lifted up, the
sovereign God, over all. So Isaiah is, as it were, ushered in a
vision into the operation-centre at the centre of the universe. It
is the Lord God Almighty's high command centre. As he looks
at God, he is told that God is on the throne. He's not enthroned
in many people's hearts and lives. There are many areas where
His will is not done on earth as it is in heaven. But it is going to
be done. God is sovereign. He is on the throne.

But this is not only a picture of His authority; it is also a
picture of His dignity: 'His train filled the temple.' It's a picture
of wonder, glory and majesty, for He is the king of the ages.

And not only that. We come to the centre of our thoughts this
evening. This God who is the God who sits on the throne, whose
train fills the temple, not only has authority and majesty but is
also possessed of absolute purity. For when Isaiah sees the
winged seraphs, each with two wings covering their faces, two
covering their feet and with two wings flying, he hears them
calling to each other, 'Holy, holy, holy is the LORD Almighty;
the whole earth is full of his glory' (6:3). In English you make a
superlative by adding the word 'most'. In Hebrew, you repeat
yourself. So 'gold, gold' means 'pure gold, the best gold'. But in
verse 6 there is something without parallel in all Hebrew lit-
erature. It is the superlative of a superlative. God is the best
holiness, He's the ultimate holiness. He is the holy, holy, holy
God. And this emphasises something that we need to recover.

One suggestion regarding the etymology of the word 'holy' is
that it derives from the root 'to cut'. When you cut, you make a

separation, a difference, a distinction. In that sense the holy God is utterly different and distinct from all that He has made. Another derivation suggests 'light' or 'brightness'. Again we can see how these two pictures come together; for God is utterly different, absolutely other than anything that we can see or know. And He dwells in unapproachable light (cf 1 Tim. 6:16). This is a picture of an absolute purity, what the theologians call His otherness, His transcendence—the fact that God is above and beyond space and time. He is the Lord God Almighty who was, and is, and is to come. He is a glorious God. And as Isaiah captures a vision of Him, we are almost at the raw edge of terror, for here is a God who is unmanageable for us human beings.

Do you remember how the children in C. S. Lewis's *The Lion, the Witch and the Wardrobe* discovered that Aslan the lion is not a tame lion—but he's good? Our God is not a tame God. People try to domesticate Him, to bring Him down to our level and make Him one of us. The heart of idolatry is to start with ourselves and project onto the back-cloth of all that there is out there, a picture of how I like to think of God. Somebody has said, we have abandoned metal images and we have created mental images; and both are idolatrous. Here is the Lord God Almighty, the Creator and Sustainer of all things. Not some cosmic influence, not some Star Wars Force to be with you, not some friendly star, not some love (whatever that might mean)—but the Holy One of Israel, always consistent with His own nature, sitting as it were on the circle of His own infinite perfections. And in His presence, the burning seraphs veil their faces and their feet. They themselves are overcome with the glory and majesty of this infinite personal holy God. Are we?

We hear an awful lot today, especially in our evangelical churches, about how we are out of touch with the world. After twenty years of pastoring evangelical churches I'm increasingly sure that we are probably more out of touch with God. I'm not denying we need to build bridges into the world, to win men and women for Christ; we need to contextualise our message and everything else. But the primary problem with most of us as individuals, and with most of our churches, is we've lost our vision of God. We are out of touch with Him. In scholarly circles, theology has become anthropology. Once it was theo-centric, God-centred; it is now anthropocentric, man-centred.

You would think, reading some modern theology, that it is man who is on the throne. That is why some people have suggested we need a Copernican revolution. Before Copernicus came along, everybody thought that the sun went round the earth. Then Copernicus said, 'No, no it's not like that at all. The earth goes round the sun,' and he revolutionised astronomy. As believers, we need a Copernican theological revolution. We need to put God back in the centre.

How can you tell? Take that heated topic, worship. How often we hear 'I like this' . . . 'I feel that' . . . 'I enjoy' . . . 'I appreciate' . . . So what? I thought worship was about what *God* appreciated. We can be so concerned about forms of worship that we actually forget that worship is what God desires and what God requires: that we ought to be giving Him the worship due to His name, as the one eternal, unique, self-existent, holy God. Do you know this God? Have you caught a vision of Him, in His being and His ways?

> Holy, Holy, Holy! Lord God Almighty!
> Early in the morning our song shall rise to Thee:
> Holy, Holy, Holy! merciful and mighty!
> God in Three Persons, blessèd Trinity!
> (Reginald Heber)

This God whom Isaiah sees is the living God. He is the God who encounters people, who comes to meet them and minister to them. We need to look up. But when we do, immediately, like Isaiah, we'll begin to find ourselves looking in.

Look in

Early this century, a philosopher-theologian called Rudolf Otto wrote a book called *The Idea of the Holy*, in which he coined the term, 'the numinous'. It means that sense of awe and terror, yet fascination, that the creature feels in the presence of the Holy One. Isaiah certainly has the numinous feeling. He has a creaturely feeling, but it is not one of smallness compared to the greatness of God. That would have been understandable; it is where world religions meet. But verse 5 is even more alarming. Isaiah doesn't feel angst at his smallness. He feels shame at his sinfulness in the presence of the absolute majesty and purity of God. Here is real guilt. We'll never know the depths of our sinfulness and shame until we have looked into the face of the Holy One of Israel, and in that light have discovered, as Isaiah did, 'Woe to me! I am ruined, I am lost, I am undone.' The root of the word seems to suggest, 'Woe is me for I am silenced.' Did you know that the gospel wants to shut your mouth?

I wasn't brought up in a committed Christian home. When I was fourteen somebody bought a Bible for me and suggested I read it. A Liverpudlian, I was a keen Everton supporter. I thought if I read three chapters a day and six at weekends God would help me and Everton Football Club. It worked; we won the Cup and in seven months I'd read the Bible from Genesis to Revelation and was feeling pretty good about myself. Then I started again, to be ready for the next season. This time, especially reading the Old Testament laws, I began to feel distinctly uncomfortable. I was only fifteen. I wasn't some big-time crook, I wasn't even a small-time crook. I didn't drink, smoke, swear or gamble. I didn't go round with bad women, or good women, or any women. I read at least three chapters of the Bible every day. I said my prayers five or six times every day. And as I read through those Old Testament laws, the fear of God got hold of my soul.

I kept telling people how good I was. I started going to church. People asked, 'Are you a Christian?' I replied, 'Sure I'm a Christian. I do this, I do that, I do the other.' And I kept telling them and telling them and telling them. My mouth hadn't been shut. But the purpose of the gospel is 'that every mouth may be silenced and the whole world held accountable to God' (Rom. 3:19).

John Newton wrote, 'T'was grace that taught my heart to fear.' Has grace done that for you? Have you been under conviction of sin? Do you know what Isaiah is encountering here? Where you know you are lost, and ruined, and helpless, and there's no hope for you—there's nothing you can do? You can always tell whether somebody's a true Christian. They've stopped talking about themselves, who they are, who they know, what they've done and what they hope to gain. They know, in the presence of this terrifying, awesome God, that they are lost. Do you? How can you dwell with such a Being who is omniscient, who knows everything, the end from the beginning, and knows all the dark secrets of your heart and mine? The hymn writer Thomas Binney captured it so well:

> Eternal Light! eternal Light!
> How pure the soul must be,
> When placed within Thy searching sight,
> It shrinks not, but with calm delight
> Can live and look on Thee.

And he takes up the seraphs:

> The spirits that surround Thy throne
> May bear the burning bliss;
> But that is surely theirs alone,
> Since they have never, never known
> A fallen world like this.

And then he turns to himself:

> Oh how shall I, whose native sphere
> Is dark, whose mind is dim,
> Before the ineffable appear,
> And on my native spirit bear
> The uncreated beam?

Here's a man who is not only coming to faith, but is on the road of faith and is being made to feel, in a crisis encounter with God, how much work there still remains to be done in his soul.

Have you ever done any house renovation? You take one little bit of plaster off, and a bit more comes with it, and before you know it you have to have the plasterer in to do the whole wall. In my experience, when you start you don't know when you're going to stop; there's no end to it. God in His mercy often meets people in crisis encounters. But, as George Verwer, I think, reminds us, 'a crisis that isn't followed by a process becomes an abscess.' There must be an ongoing coming to terms with my filthy rags of righteousness. Notice that Isaiah says, 'I am a man of unclean lips.' He was a prophet, it was his strong point, it was where his gift really lay. This was a matter of the tongue, of the lips, never mind the heart. And Isaiah says, 'Even if I start with my best point, I am undone.' As he tells us later, 'All our righteous acts are like filthy rags' (Isa. 64:6). There's no glibness here, no cheap familiarity, just an honest standing before his shame and guilt, his creatureliness, in the presence of the living God.

Look to

Thirdly, look to God's sheer grace. We are not told much about Isaiah's repentance. We are told simply of his confession. This Lord God Almighty takes the initiative—that's grace. Grace is God stepping across the dividing line between us, it is God making the first move, it is God coming to us. The live coal was taken from the altar of sacrifice, the altar of blood-offering; the altar where the sacrifice would be laid.

Michael Wilcock has reminded us several times about New Testament equivalents. You know what the New Testament equivalent of the altar is, don't you! We look back through the ages where the saints and sages trod, and we see altars reeking with the sacrifice and blood. But these were only pointers to the pastoral lamb of God.

Verse 7, 'He touched my mouth and said, "See . . ."' It's a strong prophetic word. 'Behold.' It's when God wants to grab our attention. You won't get far into the Gospel of John before you come across a similar phrase: 'See, behold, the lamb of God, who bears away the sin of the world' (John 1:29). Look on to verse 13: 'But as the terebinth and oak leave stumps when they are cut down, so the holy seed will be the stump in the land.' Here is a suggestion of God coming in mercy in a holy seed.

Go to 11:1, where we get a further clue: 'A shoot will come up from the stump of Jesse.' That which seems dead and gone, the people of Israel, those through whom the Messiah was to come, they seem to be totally devastated; God's through with them— right? Wrong. A seed will come from Jesse.

Turn over to that well-known prophetic fifty-third chapter. Verse 2: 'He grew up before him like a tender shoot, and like a root out of dry ground.' And if you want to know how the Gospel writers and the apostles dealt with Isaiah 6 you need to turn to John 12:

> For this reason they could not believe, because, as Isaiah says elsewhere: 'He has blinded their eyes and deadened their hearts, so they could neither see with their eyes, nor understand with their hearts, nor turn—and I would heal them.' Isaiah said this because he saw Jesus' glory and spoke about him. (John 12:39–41)

What does this live coal represent? The means of atonement, of forgiveness, of mercy. Sigmund Freud has done a great disservice to the human race by driving a wedge in many people's minds between sin and guilt. So now we have a society that wants to medicate its guilt-psychoses; that holds that there are people who have guilt feelings and have no reason to feel guilty. But sin and guilt, action and reaction go hand in hand in Scripture. If your guilt feelings are not a psychological warp, they are almost certainly related to your sin. People don't like that, so they cover it up. They dull the guilt with their drugs, their pleasures, their drink, their business and their busy-ness. They seek to cover it. But Isaiah says that when the live coal came from the altar he was told, 'Your guilt is taken away and your sin'—notice this word— 'atoned for.'

The Jewish Day of Atonement, *Yom Kippur*, is the day when sin is covered. That's what *kippur* means. It's the word for covering, in a holy God's presence, real, actual sin and guilt. Not simply guilt feelings, but real, shameful, vile guilt; sin against God, sin against heaven. And thank God that there is real atonement, there is a real Saviour, and His name is Jesus Christ our Lord.

Currently in the media there is a debate about asylum seekers. There's only one place where guilty sinners can find asylum, and that place is the cross of Christ, where the spotless eternal Son of God shed His own life's blood so that we might be forgiven.

> Upon that cross of Jesus
> Mine eye at times can see
> The very dying form of One
> Who suffered there for me;
> And from my smitten heart, with tears
> Two wonders I confess
> The wonders of His glorious love,
> And my own worthlessness.
> (*Elizabeth Clephane*)

Oh, the bliss of this glorious thought! My sin—not in part, but the whole—is nailed to His cross and I bear it no more. Praise the Lord, praise Lord, O my soul! Have you been to the cross for real pardon from real guilt? There on the cross the whole work is done, the whole debt is paid, and there's nothing more for guilty sinners like us to do but receive what Christ offers, and praise Him ever more.

Look out

The chapter finishes with a looking out, after Isaiah (verse 7) having been cleansed, hears God saying, 'Whom shall I send? And who will go for us?' And he says, 'Here am I. Send me.'

What is happening here happens to every redeemed heart.

'Serve God? Ha! You must be joking. I've got so much to do . . .' Well, keep your service then. Because evangelical service is born out of gospel motives, it's motivated by a heart of gratitude. 'Love so amazing, so divine, demands my soul, my life, my all.' That is the logic of the whole of Scripture.

Isaiah hears, 'Whom shall I send to other guilty, worthless, hell-deserving sinners? Whom shall I send?' And he says, 'Lord—count me in. Don't pass me by. There are so many people out there who need You, just as I've discovered Your grace. Lord please—I don't know whether You can use me or not—but if there's anything You can do with my poor pitiable life, Lord, here I am. Send me, Lord.' For, you see, 'it is by grace you have been saved, through faith–and this not from yourselves, it is the gift of God—not by works, so that no-one can boast.' (Eph. 2:8–9).

We often stop at verse 9. But verse 10 adds, 'For we are God's workmanship'—His poem, His work of art, His sculpture—'created in Christ Jesus to do good works, which God prepared in advance for us to do.' Here am I, send me. What a commission, to go to people who are going to turn their backs on the Holy Word, who are going to be hard and difficult!

And yet, out of this encounter with God, out of this rich theology, there's a 'therefore'—'Lord, here I am, available to you, *to use as and where You see fit and You see best.*' Have you ever truly prayed, 'Take my life, and let it be . . .'? Along with the grace of God is this stirring call and challenge and commission to take the gospel out.

Every school child in Liverpool used to know the famous painting by the Victorian artist Yeames which hangs in the Walker Art Gallery. It portrays a little boy being interrogated by the Roundheads during the Civil War. In an emotional set-piece, he is being asked, 'When did you last see your father?'

And this God, this holy, holy, holy God, if I'm in Jesus Christ, is my father.

When did you last see *your* Father? Come clean with your sin. Come afresh to Christ, confess it and have done with it. He who covers his sins will not prosper, but whoever confesses and forsakes them shall obtain mercy. And having laid aside the sin that clings so closely, let's afresh, looking unto Jesus, the author and the finisher of our faith, press on to the glory of our God.

'Going For The Summit'

by Mr Charles Price

Joshua 14:6–13

This address was given at the First Week's World View Meeting, and concludes with the challenge to service that has been offered for many years at such meetings at the Keswick Convention..

We have already surveyed something of the world tonight, with its vast needs, its many opportunities. We have seen graphic images of a world in desperate need. We have heard of the fantastic growth of the church in South America this century—20% of the population of Brazil would claim to be evangelical Christians, 23% of Guatamala. On the other hand we have heard of some of the stresses of being a Christian in Burma and other parts of the world like that. But we are not merely onlookers tonight, engaging in some kind of voyeurism. Every one of us in this tent tonight is a participant in God's strategy in the world. For God has so ordained matters that the only means by which He will evangelise the world is through people like you, like me. He hasn't sent angels to evangelise. He could have done of course. That would have been more effective—certainly cheaper. He has ten thousand times ten thousand, according to the count John made on one occasion; that's 100,000,000. And John said there were many others too (cf Rev. 5:11).

'Angel' means 'messenger'. Angels are waiting for God to give them instructions, but He never sends them to evangelise. If God sent angels to the mission field it would be lot cheaper at least. They wouldn't need visas or support. But He doesn't. It would be lot more effective if God were to send an angel to knock on our neighbours' doors and witness to them about

Christ. He doesn't. His strategy is that you and I knock on those door.

Of course there are enormous risks. Your neighbours know you! And you're slightly embarrassed, because they've heard you shouting at your wife through the walls once in a while, you've occasionally parked your car in front of their driveway or their door . . . You feel slightly discredited. Wouldn't it be great if an angel knocked on their door, tucked his wings behind his back, said, 'I have come to talk to you about Christ'? Don't you think they'd sit up and take notice?

But is not His strategy.

'How can they hear without someone preaching to them? And how can they preach unless they are sent?' (Rom. 10:14–15). Our concern tonight is that we understand and face, some of us perhaps for the first time, the implications that God has no strategy but me and you. That's an incredible privilege, but also an incredible responsibility. And there's not one Christian here tonight who is exempt.

The context of Joshua 14:6–13 is that Joshua is dividing up the conquered land of Canaan into portions to each of the tribes, apart from the tribe of Levi as you will know. The tribe of Judah is being assigned the southern territory.

One of their leaders, Caleb, came to Joshua, and this is essentially what he said. 'I am eighty-five years old. But forty-five years ago I came to this piece of hill territory. Then along with the other eleven spies we surveyed this part of the land. It was inhabited then by the Anakites as it is now still today. They breathed fear into my colleagues. And forty-five years ago, we turned our backs and went the other way.'

The episode is described in Numbers 13: 'We saw the Nephilim there (the descendants of Anak come from the Nephilim). We seemed like grasshoppers in our own eyes and we looked the same to them' (Num. 13:33). The Anakites were noted for being big, tall men and women like giants. But Caleb said to Joshua, 'Now forty-five years later there is a piece of unfinished business. Give me the hill territory, give me the mountain occupied by the Anakites. And with the Lord helping me,' he said, 'I'll drive them out.'

It's interesting that Caleb, an octogenarian, was planning to assault hill country, but the hill country isn't the real issue. The real issue is that the Anakites occupied it, and it had been fear of them that had sentenced the whole nation of Israel to spend the next thirty-eight years in the wilderness before entering Canaan and fulfilling the purpose and will of God for them. Caleb was motivated by unfinished business. I want to say to you, there is unfinished business in the world tonight. None of us is exempt from this. And I am going to say to you, it doesn't apply to the person next to you—it applies to you. And I know it applies to me, because Jesus Christ has a strategy for our world and there's unfinished business. And you and I are a part of that.

I want to apply the principles of this passage to our own responsibility in our world tonight. For the many years that the Keswick Convention has taken place we have met to fix our eyes on God, to understand something of who He is, something of His purpose, something of His power, of the resources He makes available to us to equip us to live a holy life—but also to fix our eyes on the needs of our world. And at the end of our meeting tonight, I'm going to challenge many of you, to whom God has already been speaking and will speak tonight, to make yourself available to God, at any time and at any cost, in the fulfilment of His unfinished business. And I shall ask you to respond publicly. All over the world there are hundreds, possibly thousands of people, who are serving God today, because here at Keswick God met with them and challenged them serve Him.

I want to draw out three simple things from this story.

He was characterised by realism

Verse 12 is not false bravado. He is not unaware of the implications of his words. There is a history to them, forty-five years in which Caleb may well have promised himself that one day he would get back to that territory where God revealed his plan and he and his colleagues failed.

In 13:1 we read what the Lord's purpose had been: He intended to give the land to the Israelites. In verse 17 ff we can see that Moses' twelve spies did a thorough job. They carried out their task and reported back to Moses (verse 27), 'Moses, everything God said about the land is true. We have never seen such fertility, such fruit. It flows with milk and honey, it's a wonderful place. But'—and how often that little word changes everything, in Scripture!—'the people who live there are powerful, the cities are fortified and very large. We even saw descendants of Anak there, the Amalekites live in the Negev, the Hittites, the Jebusites, the Amorites live in the hill country and the Canaanites live near the sea and along the Jordan' (verse 28). They said, 'The land is great, everything God said is wonderful, but Moses, you must understand something, some very strange, wild people live there.'

And ten of the spies said, 'We can't do it. The task is too great. The obstacles are too large, the force of the enemy is too overwhelming, we can't do it.' But two were different. I love what it says about Caleb in Numbers 14:24. God says, 'Because my servant Caleb has a different spirit and follows me wholeheartedly, I will bring him into the land he went to, and his descendants will inherit it.' One day I should like to write a book called, *Men of a Different Spirit*. Most of us from time to time get cold feet. But one here and one there and one somewhere else are men and women of a different spirit. And I am going to challenge you to be a man, a woman, of a different spirit tonight.

Caleb didn't have his head in the sand. He saw everything the others saw, he saw the fortified cities, he met these armies trained in warfare which he knew the Israelites, as a group of ex-slaves that had been living as nomads in the desert, were totally ill-equipped to take them on. What the other ten left out of the equation, but Caleb and Joshua didn't, was that God was in the business. 'If the Lord is pleased with us, he will lead us into that land, the land flowing with milk and honey, and will give it to us', said Joshua and Caleb (Num. 14:8), and this was what made them men of a different spirit. The obstacles certainly were great, the enemies humanly certainly overwhelming; 'If we are dependent only on human strategy and resources, then we are right to turn tail and go back into the desert. But this is God's business,' said Joshua and Caleb, 'He is going to give us the victory in that situation.'

This isn't bravado, this is realism. We need to be absolutely realistic about the world with all its need, problems, difficulties, corruption, all its antagonism to the gospel, opposition to Jesus Christ and all its down-playing of righteousness. But at the same time, we need to be utterly realistic about God, His plans, His commands, His provision, His resources.

It may be hard in the beautiful Lakeland, setting with the sun shining, to think objectively of a hurting world. Maybe you haven't even had to listen to the news this week. But escapism is not in God's plan for us. We are a minority of believers in the Lord Jesus. The moral structures are falling around about us, our leaders disappoint us with their lack of godliness and fear of God. Our children are growing up insecure, half the world if not more still goes to bed hungry every night, in desperate conditions. Violence and corruption is normal. We are no longer even shocked by it.

We need to see our world as it is. God sent the spies into Canaan with their eyes wide open. Joshua and Caleb lost the day when they came back to Kadesh Barnea and the other ten said, 'We can't do it.' Joshua and Caleb said, 'In God's strength we can,' but they lost the day and the Children of Israel spent the next thirty-eight years wandering in the wilderness until all those men over twenty, with the exception of those two, died and were buried in the desert. Now, forty-five years later, seven years into Canaan, Caleb says, 'I've not forgotten. I've not forgotten that they were bigger than we are, they made us feel like grasshoppers, they filled us with fear when we came here before. But I've also not forgotten God is on the throne. God has declared already His will to give me this territory. And I am going into the battle.' I like Caleb's mixture of past, 'The Anakites were there and their cities were large and fortified,' and future tense, 'but, the LORD helping me, I will drive them out just as he said' (Josh. 14:12). The past belongs to the Anakites, but the future tense belongs to God. 'He is my strength, He is the one who is going to give the land, just as He promised.'

I believe many of us as Christians are intimidated by the

world. We must be realistic about the world, we must come back
to God and know that no matter how threatening the world may
be, no matter how much of a losing battle we may feel that we are
fighting in seeking to serve God in the world—there are people
who go to some parts of the world and serve God for years with
never any tangible fruit—but God is doing something. Abraham
never saw what God promised him, 'But,' said Jesus, 'he saw my
day' (cf John 8:56). His sight was fixed on Christ.

He was characterised by responsibility

We need to be realistic about the needs of the world, but realistic
too that God who calls has a strategy. He's going to do something. What should be our first response when we see the needs
of the world? Is it to muster a team to go and take the world?
Caleb's first response was to find out the will of God. What has
God said about the situation? And we have seen His will expressed in Numbers 13:1. His will was that the Israelites should
occupy the land.

Now of course that was very general, and we need to begin
with understanding God's general will for the world. We know
something of this from many biblical references. Here are just
two, we haven't time for more. 'God . . . commands all people
everywhere to repent' (Acts 17:30); 'Go and make disciples of all
nations' (Matt. 28:19). No exemptions there; that's the general
will of God.

In Numbers 14:8 it's narrowed down a bit. 'Caleb and Joshua
said, "If the Lord is pleased with us, he will lead us into that land
. . . and will give it to us." ' And verse 24, 'I will bring him into
the land he went to and his descendants will inherit it.' God is
there speaking much more specifically. And now in Joshua 14:9
Caleb can say, 'So on that day Moses swore to me, "The land on
which your feet have walked will be your inheritance and that of
your children for ever, because you have followed the Lord my
God wholeheartedly." '

An understanding of God's general will thus becomes narrowed down to His specific will, so that Caleb says, 'I know that

God has promised my children, my descendants, the occupation of this land.'

You will never know the specific will of God in your life until you are living in obedience to the general will of God for your life. You can never find out 'What does God want for me personally?' until you are being totally obedient to what you know what He wants for all Christians. Some of us, especially perhaps some of us who are younger, treat God as a wonderful employment agent—'I'd like a job, give me Your will, but I'm not interested in the general will of God.' The specific will of God is revealed as we live in obedience to the general will of God.

Young person here tonight—what has conditioned your ambition? What are the seeds of your dreams and visions? Is it the will of God? Newly-married people here tonight—you have dreams of comfort, security and well-being. Are these God's plans for you? Have you asked Him, 'Father what is Your will for us now together?' Middle-aged people: what place does God have in your decision-making? The will of God is not just something to concern young people.

At any stage in life, what is God's will for my life, for my possessions, abilities, talents, gifts and resources? Maybe, even, like Caleb you are eighty-five years of age; and perhaps God said something forty-five years ago which has never yet come to pass. Maybe for you the time has come, the evening has come, to say, 'Give me this mountain.'

Someone said to me years ago, 'Never ask as your first question about anything, "Is it possible?" Ask instead, "Is it right?" If you ask "Is it possible?", then you'll live only in the realm of the possible, which is the way every man and woman on the street lives. But if you ask "Is it right?", there will be times in your life when God will show you things that will seem to you to be impossible. He will make the impossible possible.' Some of us have been intimidated as Christians. We live only in the realm of what's possible, we don't take risks, we don't go over the edge, we don't step out of the boat, much less allow God to torpedo the boat. But tonight you need to, because God is speaking to you.

One more, important, thing. True responsibility in the Chris-

tian life is not found in my promising God I'll do certain things
for Him, but in my responding to His ability. That is exactly
what Caleb did. 'This is God's business.' That's what comes
through Caleb all the way through, in Numbers and here in
Joshua. And as I respond in obedience to what He has revealed,
not taking on my shoulders the responsibility to make things
happen, only as they obeyed and trusted in God who's going to
give me the territory—God calls you to serve Him, to open your
home to somebody, to start a youth club, to found a church
somewhere, to invite some lonely neighbours into your home, to
start an Alpha course—you obey. Your responsibility in obedience then is to trust His ability to bring about what He desires.
And that's why, back in Numbers, Caleb said, 'He will lead us,
He will give us the land, it's the Lord who's with us.'

Now forty-five years later he says, 'The Lord helping me, I
will drive them out as He said—it's His will, His initiative, I'll
obey, the Lord helping me, in His strength, responding to His
abilities—things are going to happen.'

He was characterised by risk

Without risk, the will of God rarely becomes the experience of
God and you never prove what God can do with you. I'm not
talking about reckless risks of our own choosing, but those of
obedience, such as the risk Peter took when he obeyed the words
of Jesus: 'Peter got down out of the boat, walked on the water and
came towards Jesus' (Matt. 14:29). He never proved what God
could do without taking the risk.

The book of Joshua is the story of God giving the land to
Israel. It was God who gave it to them against overwhelming
odds. But every act of God in the book of Joshua, you will
discover, is precipitated by an act of obedience. 'Joshua, take the
ark of the Covenant on the shoulders of the priests and go and
stand in the Jordan river' (cf Josh. 3:14-15)—when they obeyed
what God said, He opened the waters of the Jordan river. 'Go
against the city of Jericho. March around it every day once a day
for six days, seven times on the seventh day. You obey and I will
give you the city' (cf Josh 6). Every act of God was precipitated

by obedience, and for Joshua there was risk. 'Just supposing as we march around the city they start throwing stones at us or pouring hot tar on us.'

'You obey.'

God never proves in advance what He's going to do, the provisions He's going to give and the resources He's going to make available. You never prove God sitting in an armchair with your arms folded saying, 'Come on God, do something.' Herod found that out when Jesus was brought before him and he demanded, 'Do a miracle.' He never did, and He never will in those situations. You obey; cold-blooded obedience. Caleb, Joshua, Moses, Abraham, David—all of them proved it. Right through the Bible, every time God worked there was an act of obedience which precipitated God working. You'll never know the will of God without taking risks.

And I believe we'll never be one hundred percent sure of the will of God until we are maybe eighty percent sure and step out in faith. Nearly always it's retrospectively; as you look back over your shoulder you can see, 'The Lord has led me.' But beforehand, if you're like me, you're never been one hundred percent sure—'Supposing it's wrong.'

If it is wrong, don't panic. I'll tell you why. 'Whether you turn to the right or to the left, your ears will hear a voice behind you, saying, "This is the way; walk in it." ' (Isa. 30:21). If you go wrong, don't panic. God will bring you back on track. If you worry about going wrong you never go right either. There's risk. Some of us have never taken that risk.

Obedience is not only risky, it's costly. Yet there are wonderful benefits and blessings in doing the will of God. In serving others it's far more blessed to give than to receive. And there's wonderful enrichment from serving. But there is cost, and Jesus warned we should count the cost of being a true disciple, with all that that involves.

A while ago I was visiting several countries in West Africa, and was to spend several days in Guinea speaking to a small group of about a dozen or fifteen missionaries working there. I was flown in a little plane up to the border with Liberia. The plane hadn't permission to fly over Guinea air space, so I was delivered at the border and taken across in a little dug-out canoe. On the other side someone picked me up and we drove 300 miles through the bush to the little town where the missionaries were going to meet for three or four days. I found some very godly people there, meeting in very difficult circumstances and very primitive conditions. I asked one mission leader what had been the most difficult part of the work. He said, 'Our children are all now away in college back in the home country, but when they were younger they attended school in Nigeria. Twice a year an aeroplane would come and land on the airstrip behind our home and fly them off to Nigeria. And I used to hate that air strip. I would be brave while with them, and I'd watch that little plane take off and I would watch it until it became a little speck in the sky and disappeared. And many days I'd often go and look up into the empty sky and I would weep for my children. But,' he said, and he was weeping as he told me, 'God called me. God put us here.'

Some of us don't want any cost. We want a deluxe, first-class ride to heaven. I tell you, you won't know the blessing of God, not in the way that you might know it if you were to say, 'Lord, Your will be done.' I'm not inviting you tonight to take a job in contemporary evangelical Christianity—that's nobody's business but your own. What I'm inviting you to do is to offer your body without reserve to Jesus Christ, in a way you never have before; to obey His call, His instructions, His will for your life. What He's going to do with you is His business. I understand there's somebody here who stood one night in a meeting like this at Keswick and it was thirty years before they got to the place where God eventually put them—thirty years! Now that's God's business.

I'm going to ask you tonight, as I close, to be utterly realistic about the world, the overwhelming task that we face. The obstacles that we'll meet; the minority group that we are. But at the same time, I'm going to ask you to be utterly realistic about God. He who calls you is faithful, He will do it.

I'm going to ask you to be responsible—What is the general will of God? What is the specific will of God?—and to respond to His ability, which is to live responsibly. I am going to ask you to take a risk. What risk, is God's business. And that risk, that obedience, where He leads you, He'll show you in His time.

Mr Price concluded the meeting with 'a prayer that acknowledges God's right to total lordship in our lives', and a challenge to those willing 'to go to the summit, to take the mountain' to stand up in their places as a public demonstration of that response.

'God Knows Your Need of Commitment'

by Rev. Hugh Palmer

Revelation 3:14

This address is one of a series preached at the 1996 Convention by Rev. Hugh Palmer, on the Seven Churches in Revelation.

Please imagine you're climbing on to a luxury coach and fastening your seat belts. We're off to gate-crash the celebrations at Laodicea.

It's the church's annual general meeting. The coach gets us there in time for the end of the Treasurer's report. And it's encouraging. Next we have the report of the Fabrics Committee; they are delighted to tell the members what they already know, that the new extension has been opened this past year. Then the minister reports that the membership roll is still growing, the small-group programme has been approved, and the staffing vacancies have been filled. Question time brings nothing more serious than a query about the colour of the hall carpet and a plea to keep the traditional form of the Lord's Prayer. There's a vote of thanks to the minister, the minister proposes a vote of thanks to the members, and out come the cheese and wine, the quiche and sausage rolls are brought on and the celebrations begin.

The Church Administrator's one of those people who can't resist playing with their computers. So he just checks to see if there's anything in the e-mail. There is. And the meeting has to be called back to order, because it's a message from Jesus, no doubt sending His own congratulations.

'To the angel of the church in Laodicea write: These are the words of the Amen, the faithful and true witness'—the seal of approval; that's true every time this One speaks; He is 'the faithful and true witness'. He knows. This is the report that matters.

Like everyone else, if the truth about me has to come out I prefer it to be an edited version, ideally edited by me. It's a chilling experience to listen to the real thing, and there is never a good time to hear a report like this, at least, not if you want to celebrate. They may not realised it yet at Laodicea, but this is a real party-pooper piece. As soon as the report begins it's clear that, far from their expectations, this is a church facing total rejection.

A church facing total rejection

There is no praise for the church at Laodicea. Verse 15 is enough to wipe the smile off everyone's face. The charge is, 'You are neither cold nor hot.' The Laodicean church is just like the Laodicean water. There were hot springs a few miles away bringing a constant supply. By the time it reached Laodicea, it was lukewarm. It came over the nearby cliffs in a tepid waterfall. Lukewarm water is sickening stuff with no refreshing power whatsoever. And that's their Christian faith.

'Lukewarm Christianity'. John Stott in his commentary lists these synonyms: respectable, nominal, flabby, anaemic, moderation in all things. They are not 'cold'. The word used is a strong one, meaning 'icy'. They are not hostile to the gospel, actively denying it or promoting a life-style that drives a coach and horses through it. But they are not 'hot' either. The word is also a strong one. It means 'boiling'.

Look at most modern major denominations: you'll see too much that's good and gospel about them to warrant the term 'icy cold'. But there are too many flaws for us to be honestly able to call them 'boiling hot'. You can't call a regular church-goer, who commends the faith, who recites the Creed without intending to deceive, 'icy cold' in their faith. But if that is all there is—if they are Christian enough in their outward lifestyle, but not when it comes to the crunch at any point; not when it comes to living in a way that's contrary to the accepted practices of their peer group, whether it be in factory or the office; when it comes to giving open-handedly rather than tight-fistedly; when it comes to loving the ones we don't like, who aren't our type; when it comes to naming Christ when it is costly in loss of face, loss of influence, loss of status—you can't call someone like that 'boiling hot', can you? And that is Laodicea.

What does Jesus make of them? You'd imagine that He'd be sad, wouldn't you, if that was the Christian life He viewed? That's fair enough. We might not even be surprised if He was angry. But what He says is actually stronger still. He says, 'I am about to spit you out of my mouth.' It is a strong word. 'You make me sick, I can't stomach you.' It's harsh, emotive language; not the kind of language a respectable Laodicean would have used, or a respectable Brit, come to that. We are dispassionate, unemotional, guarded. But that is not necessarily a Christian trait, and Jesus doesn't practise it. He says, 'You make me sick.' Sin doesn't leave Him neutral and disinterested. Lukewarmness leaves Him passionately concerned. When we have disputes in Christian circles and someone tells someone else off saying, 'You shouldn't speak like that of another churchgoer,' do you realise that it's rarely the strength of the language that is the problem? For we rarely use language as strong as Revelation 3:16 about each other.

However, there are a couple of things that should cause us to be careful before we do use the language of verse 16. Here's the first. *These are the words of the Amen, the true and faithful witness.* They are completely accurate, they fit the Laodicean church like a glove. But I don't have that discernment; I can't say it's true of you. That's why you must listen for yourself and check you don't suffer from their complaints. If you do, if your discipleship is lukewarm, you are told Jesus can't stomach you. But I can't say that of you. We'll come to the other reason later.

The offensiveness of being lukewarm
Jesus says that He would rather the Laodiceans were icy cold or hot than lukewarm. But what's so offensive about being lukewarm? May I suggest three things?

It's dangerous for the world A lukewarm church is about the most dangerous thing influence possible on the world around us. Please don't reduce these letters to mere attempts to sort out petty church squabbles. Jesus' mind goes beyond church walls to the world He came to save. If this congregation is hot—think of its influence, think what a beacon it'll be, think what a magnet it can be! The world never likes the church to be hot. Remember how John Wesley and those early Methodists were taunted? They were called 'enthusiasts'. But Jesus does like it hot. Oh, for more enthusiasts at Laodicea!

Cold? Why would Jesus rather they were cold? Because it would make it obvious to the world that the truth was not there, that there was not where they could find God. It would be clear to outsiders that the Laodiceans should be avoided. But if they are lukewarm, they can influence and lead astray at the same time. They can give enough religion to inoculate people against the real thing. That's why lukewarmness is so offensive. In the name of One fanatical enough to come and give His life for us, to die a barbaric, shameful degrading death for us, in the name of One who is as passionate as *that* for us—what have we done to those around us with our lukewarm religion which 'rather hopes that in due course they might find time to reflect on some of the deeper issues of life . . .'

'It turns my stomach,' says Jesus.

It's offensive to Christ Lukewarmness is offensive to Jesus Christ. There are many things in life about which it is appropriate to be moderate. But we can't be moderate about Christ. He's not a moderate person. If, when I hear the gospel, the good news of the history of Jesus, the best I can say is 'Very interesting'; if I can't get much further than putting a fish badge on my lapel, if that's all . . . I'm not asking for everyone to stand on soap boxes. I'm simply saying, we can't owe someone our lives and be lukewarm.

An American soldier was killed under fire in Vietnam rescuing a trapped and wounded comrade. Several years later his parents invited the rescued man, whom they had never met, to their home for a meal; they wanted to get to know the person for whom their son had given his life. It was a disastrous evening. The soldier arrived for the meal an hour late—never a good start. He turned out to be coarse, rude and offensive, and utterly ungrateful when speaking about their son. As they closed their door on him at the end of the evening, the mother just turned to her husband and said, 'Why did our son have to give his life for someone so rude and ungrateful?'

Of course, we're like the Laodiceans. We're punctual, we do not arrive late. We're polite, not rude. But if the Father looked down from heaven, would He be looking at us and saying, 'Why did My Son have to give His life for the likes of him or her? So ungrateful—just lukewarm?'

It's deceitful to ourselves This is perhaps the most striking reason given here. Tepid, moderate Christians are an even bigger danger to themselves than they are to anyone else. Look at verse 17: 'You say, "I am rich; I have acquired wealth and do not need a thing." But you do not realise that you are wretched, pitiful, poor, blind and naked.' Laodicea was a wealthy town. When it was devastated by an earthquake in 60 AD, the Laodiceans rebuilt the city without a government grant or empire subsidy. They were proud of that. And as so often, the spirit of the world creeps into the church and pride is infectious. Laodicea was proud of its location, its tradition, its heritage and its name. Does that ring any bells with churches you might know?

Our long-established British historic denominations often seem proud of their riches. They speak proudly of their history, their traditions. I've been inside evangelical church buildings which are shrines, at a certain level, to some great one of the past—two or three have what look very like relics there to prove it. And it can all blind us to the reality of the present.

Laodicea was a city full of banks. Jesus says, 'You are poor.' Laodicea was famous for its medical school and its eye salves. Jesus says, 'You are blind.' Laodicea had many clothing factories. Jesus says, 'You are naked.' Lukewarm, mutual admiration societies sipping coffee, complimenting each other—their feel-good factor is high. 'You make me sick,' says Jesus.

It's easy to be rich and respectable; much, much harder to be rich and radical, to step out of line. It's easy to be rich and interested in spiritual things. That's fair enough; you can go to church, you can come to Keswick. But it's hard to be rich and hot, to be an enthusiast.

Jesus' judgements are very startling. I've been struck afresh by that as we've looked at these letters. Who would think the feeble churches could be so strongly commended? And who would think the big-name churches could be so strongly condemned? The lesson for us is clear. We have constantly to keep ourselves under His word, and ask ourselves, 'What does Jesus think?'

Because it is not what I naturally think.

A church offered total restoration

I'm still reeling from the shock of Jesus' outrageous language when I run into another shock. He is not going to close the church down.

That's what I'd do if I felt as He does about a place, and if I were the lord of the church and just had to snap my fingers and that would be an end of it. They make Him sick—yet He wants them back, and He offers total restoration. Verse 18, 'I counsel you'—notice how gentle He is; so churned up about them at one level, He doesn't command them, He doesn't snap at them, He has advice for them, vital, saving advice—'I counsel you to buy from me gold refined in the fire, so that you can come become rich.'

In America, a rich man committed suicide. In his pocket were found $30,000 and a letter. 'I've discovered during my life that piles of money do not bring happiness. I'm taking my life because I can no longer stand the solitude and boredom. When I was an ordinary workman in New York, I was happy. Now I possess millions, I'm infinitely sad and prefer death.' He had discovered the hollowness of the wealth in the banks of Laodicea.

I was speaking to someone this morning who had lost far more than the $30,000 found on this man; and he told me, 'It's all right. We know where our true riches are, in Jesus.'

'I counsel you,' says Jesus, 'to buy from me . . . white clothes to wear.' Laodicea was famous for its black wool. But here are white clothes to wear, 'so that you can cover your shameful nakedness.' They hadn't even realised there was anything wrong. And when they did, what could they do about it?

I'd be very surprised if I were the only person in the tent this afternoon who can look back at a time, long before I was a Christian, when I was quite happy with life and certainly quite happy with myself. The turning point for me was when I came across a Christian friend and was attracted by his life. I wanted to be like him, and then I discovered I couldn't be. And far from being content with life I was now asking. 'How can I get a life that's worth living?' 'Come to me,' says, Jesus, 'buy from me . . . white clothes to wear, so you can cover your shameful nakedness; and salve to put on your eyes, so that you can see.' Wake up to the condition you are in, He says.

Probably the greatest miracle is when God's word suddenly makes sense to us. Only God can give us the eyes to see and understand. When He began to make sense of His word to me, He began to make sense of the world to me; He began to make sense of life and eternity. Remember, this is 'the ruler of God's creation' (verse 14) who speaks. It has the sense of 'the originator of creation'. He can deliver. The one who can make our ordered world out of the chaos with which it began can turn a lukewarm Christian into a hot one.

'Those whom I love I rebuke and discipline' (verse 19). Can you get over that? I find this jumble of emotions very moving. He faces these people, for whom He sacrificed, to whom He is committed, for whom He longs, who turn His stomach—yet He still loves them. And that's the other reason why we should be careful before we speak in the language of verse 16. If you are going to speak as Jesus speaks in verse 16, you need to love like the Jesus of verse 19. Those of us who are best at being party-poopers aren't normally very good at verse 19. We want to condemn.

Jesus speaks harshly to save, to warn, to discipline, to rebuke, so that people will turn, be earnest and repent. 'Here I am! I stand at the door and knock. If anyone hears my voice . . .' (3:20).

You can see where His heart, is can't you! The church, the congregation as a whole might not turn, but this is for the individual. '. . .If anyone hears my voice and opens the door, I will come in and eat with him, and he with me.' 'Eat' speaks of the main meal of the day, it's the mark of a relationship restored. He can't face the thought of them one moment, He looks at lives that disgust Him; and then He offers to come and share food with them. It makes you want to say, "Thank you, Jesus. What a Saviour!"

It doesn't stop there. This is total restoration. Verse 21: 'To him who overcomes, I will give the right to sit with me on my throne, just as I overcame and sat down with my Father on his throne.' He's looking to the future. Oh, He's our guest now, He comes as the King of heaven, but we will be His guests then, on the throne room of heaven—if we are those who overcome.

'Just as I overcame,' says Jesus, 'and sat down with my Father on his throne.' Jesus made His way to glory via the shame of the cross. The Laodiceans will make their way to glory via the shame of repentance. For that's the other message for this church.

A church needing total repentance

At the heart of verses 19–20 is a command: 'Be earnest, and repent.' Turn around, do a U-turn. This church is heading one, way and Jesus says, 'Turn round. Come with Me the other way. And then be earnest, be zealous, be hot.'

'Here I am, I stand at the door and knock.' See, they are in a service, they gather together, they are excited: 'This is it, this is what it's all about!' If they had Anglican liturgy in those days they would be saying the response, 'The Lord is here, His Spirit is with us.' Then comes the knock; and for all the talk of 'The Lord is here and His Spirit is with us,' He's not; He's outside. Imagine the horror of it. Imagine trying to come to terms with it. 'We've been meeting week after week, month after month, year after year, talking as if God's here with us and what a wonderful privilege it is'—and He's outside.

I remember the night when God reached out and grabbed hold of me. That Christian friend whose life had so impressed me was in my bed-sit and we were having a cup of coffee together. He turned round in his chair, looking rather embarrassed, and asked me the question that found me out. He said, 'Hugh—you've never really said. Where do you stand with Christ?'

There'd be no point asking the Laodiceans that question. They'd answer, 'Fine, just where we need to be.' But they discovered there was a much worse question to be asked. 'Where does Christ stand with you?' That's the one that matters. That's the one that turned the Laodicean church upside down. If they were going to repent, they needed to swallow the shame of admitting that they'd got it wrong all the time.

It's hard to have a spiritual pedigree, to be church-going, Keswick Convention-going, whatever it is, and to face verse 20. Some friend may say, '*You* don't need to worry, surely you're all right.' It's hard to be rich and hot, to be rich and to risk. And yet Jesus commands us to be.

We are coming to the end now. I'm going to ask in a moment that we be quiet and just think on what this message has for us. 'If anyone hears my voice . . .'—if for some that voice has been speaking of something of which we need to repent, I'm going to ask in the silence for those people just to stand, as a sign of repentance.

There's nothing magic in standing up. If we are never willing to stand out in a crowd, how will we ever be hot for Jesus? Especially in a friendly crowd like this. I have to admit, I'm a reserved Brit. I find it easy to wince when people get hot for Jesus. Well, just standing up isn't being hot for Jesus. It often looks over the top to me and probably it is sometimes, but passionate obedience to Christ rarely conforms to social expectations. To be lukewarm and respectable—that's easy. But to be hot, to be boiling for Jesus, may mean we can't be respectable any more.

So do you need to repent? Is that voice mentioning something specific? A relationship that needs sorting out? Money and generosity that needs working out? A prayer life that needs attending to? A willingness to be known as a Christian? Some sacrificial service? I don't whether it was anything specific for the

Laodiceans. There's nothing mentioned here, just an attitude. They had to deal with a pride that would acknowledge Jesus but not be dependent on Him, that would dabble in Christianity but not be zealous for it, that would be lukewarm but not boiling. Is that the attitude of which we need to repent? Are you listening? 'He who has an ear, let him hear what the Spirit says to the churches.'

Let's be quiet for a moment or two. And in that quiet, if God's speaking to you or calling to you, either over something specific or a general attitude; if it's time you moved from being lukewarm to being boiling hot for Him—I ask you simply to stand, where you are, and in a few moments I'll lead us in a prayer.

'The Water of Life'

by Rev. Alex Ross

John 4:1–42

Earlier this year I was in India as one of three English contributors to a Bible Exposition Week organised by Operation Mobilisation in Hyderabad, which was funded in part by the generous gift sent from Keswick last year. Some of the 250 pastors who attended had travelled for four days on buses and trains to get to Hyderabad, so they really meant business. They came from tough backgrounds. One told me he arrived in a town to plant a church and for the first three months slept in the bus station before he could get a room. Now he has a room and he's looking to build a church in that town. There are great things happening in India. They never give any official statistics, it's too sensitive a situation. But I sense that it's going well, and an event like that is of real use to the church. They are going to have another one next year, to equip these men in preaching. Let's go on praying!

One quite remarkable thing about India is the difference between some of the very dry parts of the country and the green areas you find in them—farms, plantations, gardens. Of course, the secret is that there is water present. Water transforms any landscape (which I assume is why it's so green up here in the Lake District . . .)

What is true physically is also true spiritually. Tonight we are going to look at Jesus' offer of living water which totally changed the landscape of one person's life. When John the Baptist was preparing people for Jesus' arrival, he said that there were two things that Jesus was going to do when He came. He pointed to

Jesus and said, 'Look, the Lamb of God, who takes away the sin of the world! (John 1:29), and called him 'he who will baptise with the Holy Spirit' (John 1:33). Those are the two things every member of the human race needs: forgiveness for our sins and a new power to live by. Jesus came to be our Saviour to save us from sin, and He came to baptise us with the Holy Spirit. On Tuesday we considered the cross, and we saw how forgiveness is possible for all of us day by day, as we keep returning to Christ our Saviour. Now tonight we are going to look at the Holy Spirit, the new power we have to live by.

Of course the New Testament doesn't normally separate these two works of Christ, they very much come together. And here in John 4 the living water is eternal life; the living water is salvation; and the Holy Spirit is vital in both these areas. Salvation is impossible without the work of the Spirit. Life is impossible without us having God's Spirit in our lives.

We are going to highlight the work of the Holy Spirit as we see Him here in John 4. There are five things about Jesus' offer of living water which make this the most exciting offer in the world. Our society is full of special offers, unique offers, fantastic offers, free offers. Every day the papers are full of them. But we are going to see the difference that Jesus' offer of living water made to one person. Not only did it change the landscape of one woman, it also changed the town in which she lived. One of the features of this living water is that when it begins to flow things start to happen.

If ever the church needed the movement of God's Spirit it needs it, I believe, in the United Kingdom today in 1996. Our society desperately needs this living water at this time. John's Gospel was written so that our faith in Christ may increase: 'Jesus did many other miraculous signs in the presence of his disciples, which are not recorded in this book. But these are written that you may believe that Jesus is the Christ, the Son of God, and that by believing you may have life in his name' (20:30). I hope tonight as we look at John 4 that our faith in Christ will grow. Faith is not just like a dollop of mashed potatoes that we get on our plates when we become Christians. It is dynamic, it's growing as we go on in the Christian life. I hope that in John 4 we will see more of Christ, and more of what He wants to give us in the living water.

Living water is for everybody

The original offer was made in the country of Samaria, in the town of Sychar, at a place called Jacob's Well. People had been stopping there for centuries. It was a kind of motorway service-centre, where people would pull in on their journey and get what was on offer.

It was rather unusual in this place to see a Jew talking, as Jesus was talking, to a Samaritan. The Jews regarded Samaritans as half-breeds. Today they would have used the term 'ethnic cleansing'. The Samaritans were unacceptable racially because they'd intermarried with other nations, politically because they'd compromised with other countries, and religiously because they were pluralists. So for Jesus to be talking with this woman was rather like a Unionist and a Republican talking together in Northern Ireland, or a Hindu and a Muslim in Kashmir, or a Serb and a Croat in Sarajevo. The woman was certainly surprised (verse 9): ' "You are a Jew and I am a Samaritan woman. How can you ask me for a drink?" (For Jews do not associate with Samaritans.)' By talking to her Jesus was breaking through some of the barriers of His day and ignoring some of the big 'isms' of His society—racism, sexism, Judaism. Even more, we know from our reading that this woman was a moral outcast. We talk about the Good Samaritan; we could call this lady the Bad Samaritan.

But none of these things, as we look at the story, stop the water from flowing, because in verse 10 Jesus makes this woman an offer she can't refuse. ' Jesus answered her, "If you knew the gift of God and who it is that asks you for a drink, you would have asked him and he would have given you living water." ' He longs to give this woman spiritual life. He is longing for her to ask for God's gift, He is longing to give her living water. Jesus is never the reluctant giver. He is the very opposite.

If you were organising a 'Living Water Tour' for Jesus and were making a list of the type of people who you thought would benefit from meeting Christ—people who would be receptive and open to the Holy Spirit, people who would want more of God in their lives—I don't think you'd have put this woman on your list. She doesn't seem the Holy Spirit type, she wouldn't come to Keswick. She wouldn't be in your local church. Which, I suppose, is a reminder to us that there are no 'Holy Spirit types'. Everybody in the world is a Holy Spirit type. Everybody needs the living water. We are all in need of God's power in our lives.

Jesus picks this up later. People and places, He tells us are not going to be important any more. Verse 21: 'Believe me, woman, a time is coming when you will worship the Father neither on this mountain nor in Jerusalem.' Mount Gerazim won't matter. Jerusalem won't matter. The living water is going to flow right around the world. People are going to be worshipping God everywhere. It's not going to be confined to one special place.

So will it be just a general free-for-all—plumb into God and get a blessing, a New Age type of experience without principles? Not according to Jesus. In verse 22 He points to some important origins. 'You Samaritans worship what you do not know; we worship what we do know, for salvation is from the Jews.' He is anchoring His offer in history. Salvation comes from the Jews. The Old Testament is written by Jews, for Jews, about Jews. The New Testament was written by Jews, and is about Jews—Jesus was a Jew. So you see why Jesus says salvation is from the Jews, and why Christians are always going back to the Bible, and why Keswick is built around a Bible teaching ministry: it is because it takes us back to the source of our salvation. It takes us back to Jesus, it makes sure we are on the right track, for where would we be if we didn't go back to the source? That is why it is so important to open the Bible, to meet the real Christ.

But Jesus is showing this woman that nationality now has no advantage. Verses 23–24: 'Yet a time is coming and has now come when the true worshippers will worship the Father in spirit and truth, for they are the kind of worshippers the Father seeks. God is spirit, and his worshippers must worship in spirit and in truth.' Living water affects us in terms of truth and in terms of the way we live. We live by the truth, we live by the Spirit.

It's significant that Jesus brings, and keeps, these two together, for as Christians we have a habit of polarising them. Some Christians are very strong on the word and on truth, and tend to despise too much emphasis on the Spirit. Other Christians are really keen on the Spirit and on power and on excitement, and tend to neglect the truth. But Jesus keeps both emphases firmly together here.

David Watson back in the 1970s summed up what Jesus is saying here. 'All truth and we dry up. All Spirit and we blow up. But Spirit and truth—and we grow up.' It is happening all over the world. Last night we heard about 60,000,000 evangelical Christians in South America. A hundred years ago there were no Christians in Korea; I was talking to two Koreans this morning who told me that 15% to 20% of the population is Christian.[1] Tonight there are millions of Christians on every continent who would stand up and say that Jesus has transformed their lives. It happened to me many years ago, it happened to you, it can happen to our neighbours, it can happen on the streets where we live, it can happen wherever the living waters start to flow. Don't let's limit God. What Jesus teaches us in John 4 is that the Holy Spirit is for everybody, not just confined to a few.

The living water is for the world.

Living water is abundant

Water in the Middle East is always precious, but water at midday in the Middle East is even more precious. It's what everybody wants and needs. And Jacob's Well was the place to get it. We are told in verse 11 that the well was deep. Though it was a dug-out, there was an underground spring which made it reliable then, and it's still being used today. So this well is a fabulous illustration of what Jesus is offering.

But the woman has yet to understand that Jesus is offering

---

1. As of 1993 Seoul, capital of South Korea, was almost 40% Christian, with over 7,000 churches, and was home to 10 of the largest congregations in the world (Patrick Johnstone, *Operating World*, O M Publishing, 5th edn 1993, p. 337)

something greater than what she's been used to from Jacob's Well. Look at verse 12: 'Are you greater than our father Jacob, who gave us the well and drank from it himself, as did also his sons and his flocks and herds?' After all, this woman was thinking, this well has been satisfying the needs of people for over 1,500 years.

So Jesus goes on to explain what He means. He replies, 'Everyone who drinks this water will be thirsty again.' He is saying what everyone knows: water from Jacob's Well isn't totally satisfying. No water is. Pay extra for expensive mineral water and it doesn't quench your thirst any longer than tap water does. But, He continues (verse 14), 'whoever drinks the water I give him will never thirst. Indeed, the water I give him will become in him a spring of water welling up to eternal life.'

Throughout the Bible water is used as a picture of spiritual life. Psalm 36:8–9—'You give them drink from your river of delights. For with you is the fountain of life'; Isaiah 12:3—'With joy you will draw water from the wells of salvation'; Isaiah 55:1—'Come, all you who are thirsty, come to the waters'; Jeremiah 2:13—the Lord is 'the spring of living water'; in Ezekiel 47, the river of life is flowing from the temple of God; Revelation 21:6—'To him who is thirsty I will give to drink without cost from the spring of the water of life.' So water in biblical terms is a good picture of the spiritual life that God wants to give, because in a country like Israel water keeps people alive, quenches thirst, satisfies, brings growth and cleans people up. All these are the things that Jesus came to do. He wants to pour His Holy Spirit into people's lives in such a way that we will be taken right into eternity.

So Jesus isn't talking about just a few drops. As I speak, advertisements in the London Underground promoting the Water Company are showing huge pipes with people walking around inside them. That's only a drainpipe in comparison to what Jesus is talking about here! In verse 14, we see that it is 'a spring of water welling up to eternal life'.

Now a spring has life of its own. It flows on despite the weather, it is always bubbling away. And this is what happens when God comes into our lives; He brings a life of His own. He is not affected by circumstances. He has the power to take us to heaven.

The spring that God puts in our lives will never be turned off. Jesus is telling us that it is an eternal spring that will go on for ever. When God comes to live in our lives, we have an eternal source of refreshment. And this is of course what we need; this is what our society desperately needs at the moment. This is what people are looking for, this source of spiritual life that will bubble up and satisfy and never be taken away. That's what Jesus offers, to those of us who belong to Him. He wants this well there to be satisfying us day by day. It's not just for Keswick or for Sundays. It's a moment-by-moment experience. It's a bubbling spring.

Living water brings conviction

The woman recognised a good offer when she saw one. 'Sir, give me this water so that I won't get thirsty and have to keep coming here to draw water' (verse 15). Unfortunately she missed the point. She had taken Jesus literally.

Jesus was interested in her physical needs; look at the next verse. 'He told her, "Go, call your husband and come back." ' He didn't hedge around, he went straight for the jugular. He pointed to the greatest need in her life. You remember He did the same with Nicodemus the great religious leader; the first thing He said to him was, 'You must be born again' (John 3:7).

So how did this woman react? She made her shortest statement of the whole conversation. She said, 'I have no husband.' Technically she was right, though she was obviously trying to prevent any further probing into this particular aspect of her life. But she doesn't realise who she's up against. She's about to learn.

Verse 17: 'Jesus said to her, "You are right when you say you have no husband. The fact is, you have had five husbands and the man you now have is not your husband." ' Jesus knew every detail of her life, her failures, her mistakes. Any woman who had five husbands must have had a sense of failure. Most people I've met with just one failed marriage are full of regret and wish it could have been different.

Interestingly, Jesus doesn't condemn her. He exposes her sin, but He doesn't judge her. But He does want her to know that He knows. And immediately she comes under conviction. Isn't it important that when God speaks the word does break into our lives—that God does bring a sense of failure and guilt and uncertainty, which never grows less however long we are a Christian? I've been a Christian just over twenty years now and I find I don't feel any less guilty than when I first became a Christian. In fact I may feel more guilty.

Jonathan Edwards wrote this twenty years after his conversion:

> I have had very affecting views of my own sinfulness and vileness; very frequently to such a degree, as to hold me in a kind of loud weeping . . . so that I have often been obliged to shut myself up. I have had a vastly greater sense of my own wickedness, and the badness of my heart, than ever I had before my conversion . . . . And it is affecting to think, how ignorant I was, when a young christian, of the bottomless, infinite depths of wickedness, pride, hypocrisy and deceit, left in my heart. (*Personal Narrative*)

Jonathan Edwards was a big preacher, one of the great saints of the past. But if the work of God's Spirit is going to be in our lives there will always be conviction.

We wouldn't pour clean water into a dirty glass or a rusty kettle. God is always having to clean up our lives because we are always dirty, we are always soiled; and God and sin don't mix. God's Spirit does not work in a moral vacuum, and where the living water is flowing, there would be conviction. That's why we can never talk about Jesus the baptised without talking about Jesus the Saviour; that's why we cannot talk about conviction without also talking about filling. This is part of what God is doing here. As the word of God is spoken in the power of the Spirit, so there will be conviction.

Living water is radical

As you read these verses you find that people are rearranging their schedules because of the living water. In verse 28 the woman left her jar at the well and went back to get the water. In verses 31–33, Jesus doesn't have His lunch. In verse 40 He rearranged His timetable so that He could stay on for a few more days. And just as the woman was surprised that Jesus was talking to her, so too were the disciples. Verse 27: 'Just then his disciples returned and were surprised to find him talking with a woman.' They recognised she was a woman. They recognised she was a Samaritan. And they probably recognised she was a tart.

Then in verse 28, she left the water jar and went back to the town. That just has to be the detail of an eye-witness. It's a terrific visual aid for what this lady had to do. Up until then all she'd been interested in doing was filling her jar with water from Jacob's Well. But now she'd met Jesus Christ that was secondary. The water jar until now had been fundamental to her survival. But now it's replaced with another priority. Suddenly her whole world view is changed. It's not the water from the well that's important now but the water from Jesus. Now that *is* radical!

So what does she do? 'Leaving her water jar, the woman went back to the town and said to the people, "Come, see a man who told me everything I ever did. Could this be the Christ?" ' What a statement: 'He told me everything I ever did.' Yet as far as we know, Jesus only told her that she had five husbands and that the man she was now living with was not her husband. But perhaps that's all she ever did; perhaps that's all she ever lived—men and sex. If that's so then the people of the town must have been surprised to hear her talking so openly, because women like this don't normally talk about what they do, though everybody wonders what they do.

Jesus has broken through all that. He has got to the heart of her life, because He has spoken to her about her deepest need. This is what happens when we read the Bible, listen to a sermon, listen to other Christians; God can speak to us through His word and penetrate.

C. H. Spurgeon the nineteenth-century preacher had finished

his sermon. A little girl said to her mother, 'How does he know what goes on in our house?' That's what the woman discovered: that Jesus knew what was going on in her house and couldn't keep quiet about it. Look at the impact of her testimony 'They came out of the town and made their way towards him' (verse 30). 'Many of the Samaritans from that town believed in him because of the woman's testimony, "He told me everything I ever did." ' (verse 39).

The disciples had gone into the same town to get lunch, and that's what they'd come back with. The woman went into the town, and came back with all these people. That's what happens when people have asked for the living water; suddenly the water begins to flow in their lives. The woman hadn't been on a course, she hadn't attended a special programme on training for evangelism; but she had been with Jesus, she had asked for the living water, and it radically changed her.

Sometimes our lives are so jammed with the water jars and trivia of life, that we actually don't talk about Christ. We are not bringing people to Jesus.

In the Canadian timber industry, logs sometimes jam while being floated down the river to the sawmill. One of the best ways of releasing the log-jam and the tremendous pressure it creates is to is to raise the level of the water. Then the logs begin to move again. That's what we need sometimes in our lives; we need more of God's living water, we need more of the Lord. That's what we need when sometimes we have log-jams in our churches: to be giving our lives more to Christ, to have more of His Spirit flowing through our gatherings. We need to leave our water jars, we need to get our priorities back in order, we need to see where these priorities are so that can begin to speak to the world.

What made this woman so radical that she couldn't keep quiet? The living water was flowing through her life. Jesus was just the same; He couldn't keep quiet either. Verse 6—He was tired, it was mid-day, the sun was hot, but it couldn't stop Him talking to this woman. Verse 31—the disciples returned from the town with lunch but Jesus wasn't interested. Why? Jesus gives the answer in verse 32: 'But he said to them, "I have food to eat that you know nothing about."' The disciples were confused.

'Could someone have brought him food?' Not at all. In verse 34 Jesus tells them that sharing the water of life was more important than His lunch. That was His priority.

In verse 35, Jesus re-writes the way we normally look at things. 'Do you not say, "Four months more and then the harvest"? I tell you, open your eyes and look at the fields! They are ripe for harvest.' You see, normally you harvest once a year. No, Jesus is saying: it's harvest all the time, every day, week, month—you don't have to wait till September or October. The woman couldn't wait to go and tell people. She didn't wait for a committee meeting, or until she'd got some new technique of sharing the gospel. Jesus says, 'Open your eyes, look at the people of the world.' Every day we see thousands of people on television, we drive past thousands of people in our cars, we walk past thousands of people in the street—we're surrounded by people. And Jesus says, 'Open your eyes and look at the fields! They are ripe for harvest.'

The church where I work in North London is right in the middle of a busy shopping area. Most weeks we try to go out on the streets to give out leaflets and to talk to people. Every time we go out, we find someone who is interested and wants to hear more: someone who wants to receive. It's true; the fields are ripe for harvest. And Jesus says, 'Open your eyes.' You don't have to wait for Billy Graham to come back. You don't have to wait to be given a book to pass on. 'Open your eyes', says Jesus. That's what's happening here in John 4. As the living water flows, people start talking and believing.

But Jesus does not only mean that some people are ready to respond. Some are actually near the final harvest. Hardly a week passes but that we see people dying unexpectedly, being taken out of the fields of life.

This is very urgent. It is an emergency. That's why Jesus went without His lunch, why He stayed on there a few more days, why He talked when He was tired, why the woman left her water jar because suddenly the enormity of the situation was breaking in on her. The living water is radical. We can't just talk about being filled with the Holy Spirit, unless we expect it to change us and to begin to move us out into the fields to talk as this woman did.

Living water is for individuals

As Jesus comes to the end of His conversation with this woman He lets her know who He really is. She raises the subject of the Messiah, verse 25, and in verse 26 Jesus declares, "I who speak to you am he."

Before the woman can receive the living water, she needs to know who Jesus is personally. And that is true of every person who is going to know God's Spirit in their lives. We do have to come to Jesus. Jesus invites us to come. 'Jesus stood and said in a loud voice, "If anyone is thirsty, let him come to me and drink. Whoever believes in me, as the Scripture has said, streams of living water will flow from within him." ' (John 7:38).

So while there are thousands of us here tonight, there still has to be a personal response. There has to be a personal encounter between you and Jesus. I can't do it for you, your wife can't do it for you, your minister can't do it for you.

Paul said to us, 'Be filled with the Spirit' (Eph. 5:18). It's written in the present continuous tense. It's something I believe we all have to keep seeking from God, because we all leak. And we all need to keep coming back to God and asking Him to fill us again with this living water.

Malcolm Muggeridge wrote this:

I may, I suppose, regard myself or pass for being a relatively successful man. People occasionally stare at me in the streets—that's fame. I can fairly easily earn enough to qualify for admission to the highest slopes of the Inland Revenue—that's success. Furnished with money and a little fame even the elderly, if they care to, may partake of trendy diversions—that's pleasure. It might happen once in a while that something I said or wrote was sufficiently heeded for me to persuade myself that it represented a serious impact on our time—that's fulfilment. Yet I say to you—and I beg you to believe me—multiply these tiny triumphs by a million, add them all together, and they are nothing—less than nothing, a positive impediment—measured against one draught of that living water Christ offers to the spiritually thirsty, irrespective of who or what they are. (Sermon, '*Living Water*', *1968*)

The woman of John 4 would have agreed with Malcolm Muggeridge, that this living water radically altered and changed her life. It made two main differences. The first is that she was confronted with her life and she was confronted with her failure. And the second was that it made her a witness. From the moment she asked for living water, her life was opened to the truth and her mouth was opened to speak.

And aren't those the two things that our church desperately needs today? An awareness of sin that leads to holiness, and a boldness for Christ that leads to evangelism. And if we want to be holy, and if we want to be witnesses, then Jesus shows here in John 4 that it happened for this woman. She became aware of her sin and she became a witness.

'The Disgrace of Pretence'

by Rev. David Coffey

Matthew 23

Janet is not only my wife but my friend. Through thirty years we've had some very honest and truthful conversations with one another which have led to changes in our relationship. We share in common a love for the greatest Friend we could ever have. And I want to say to you, sisters and brothers, that this greatest Friend desires this evening to have with many of us a deeply personal conversation. It's going to marked by honesty; it's going to be marked by truthfulness; and it is going to lead to changes in our relationship with Him. This week we have said many things to Jesus in song: truthful things, beautiful things, wonderful things about that relationship. And every time we open God's word, it's as if Jesus has said, 'I have heard your songs, and I receive your songs; but I want to speak to you honestly and truthfully.'

I believe the Divine Physician is asking us to come into His surgery this evening and to treat some of us, because we have become very sick, because of unconfessed and unrecognised sin. We are saying, much as we might do to an earthly physician, 'I'm fine.' And He says to us, 'You're not.'

But the best news you're going to hear in the doctor's surgery this evening is that there is a cure for what troubles you.

Maybe you belong to a congregation that is spiritually sick because of unrecognised and unconfessed sin. And you say to the Lord this evening, 'Lord, we're really fine.' The Divine Physician wants to come and say, 'You are not. You are suffering greatly from spiritual sickness. You can't really sing "Shine,

Jesus, shine . . . Flow, river, flow . . . Blaze, fire, blaze"—You can't sing things like that so long as you persist in this spiritual sickness. But I have the remedy.'

As we turn to Matthew 23 we find an extremely ugly picture. God is going to use it to speak to us this evening; some of us perhaps in the early stages of sin-sickness, others in a fairly long-term state of unconfessed sin. But the Divine Physician is going to persist with us this evening. And He says to you at the outset, 'By My grace at work within you there is a cure, there is a remedy.' And of course His medicine, as always, will be repentance. I give you warning; this is the antibiotic He wants you to take.

The great Puritan Thomas Watson talked of repentance like this. You have to have a sight of sin, a sorrow for sin, a confession of sin, a shame of sin, a hatred of sin, and a turning from sin. All that makes up the medicine of repentance. And just as a doctor might say to you, 'You must persist in the taking of this antibiotic, even though you feel better when you first begin to take it; drain the bottle dry, empty that bottle of tablets,' so God wants the full dosage of medicine of repentance as He exposes the sin-sickness in our lives and in our churches, in order that we might be those healthy communities, lights to the world. That's the only reason we're here this evening. We're not here for self-indulgence. We are here as sick patients in God's surgery, so that people might be made well to go out and others might know the cure for sin.

So Jesus talks to us from His word, from Matthew 23, about the disgrace of pretending.

It's a very serious disorder. Have you ever seen such righteous anger from a loving Saviour? 'Woe!' He says. Seven times these references to hypocrisy, five times a reference to blindness, once to snakes and vipers. They are like thunder and lightning strikes; they come from a loving heart but they are spoken with such earnestness and such passion. This is the wrath of the Lamb, directed against His bride the church. He moves us towards that day when we will be spotless, without any wrinkle, any uncleanness, any sickness about us. But He desperately desires to reach a needy world, and in order to do that the bride of Christ has to be healthy. That's why we are in the doctor's surgery this evening. That's why He names this malady, this serious disorder, as a disgrace of pretence.

Now originally it came to a group of religious leaders who were rotten at the core, though not all of them; in the Gospels it's recorded that a scribe asked Jesus about the way to life, and Jesus said to him, 'You are not far from the kingdom.' So don't write off all the scribes and Pharisees as you hear Him talking in this language to them here. This morning we heard from Stuart Briscoe the first of our studies on God's ten words. But out of those ten words these scribes and Pharisees had made a system embracing fifty volumes and 6,000 rules. The scribes wrote the volumes and the Pharisees kept the rules. It was a system for getting right with God. They actually thought it pleased God; but you can see what Jesus says about it in verse 4 about it: it simply put a burden on people's backs. And they didn't lift a finger to remove it.

And again and again from 23:13 the word 'hypocrite' appears. It's the word from which we get our word 'actor'. It means somebody who learns the lines and puts on a disguise and make-up. They're playing a part, it's not the real them. That's what a hypocrite, a pretender, is. It's not the real thing. And the Divine Physician comes this evening and says—yes, in love, but also in righteous, jealous anger—'Hypocrites.' Pretending is never solitary. Hypocrisy and blindness are linked together in this chapter, because they were both blind guides. It wasn't simply that they were acting a part, that it was just them that was at fault. The whole system was being affected.

Malachi brings this out beautifully. He shows us people who have allowed cynical faith to be corrupted into cynical approaches to worship, and have lost sight of what the whole purpose is: 'My name will be great among the nations.' And the people sniff contemptuously and say, 'What a burden!' (cf Mal. 1:12ff). When there's that attitude in the hearts of religious leaders it's infectious. Malachi says that descendants will be rebuked (2:3); he means that the young people will not want to follow in that tradition. Worshippers soon pick up the heart of what's really happening.

So Jesus talks about this disgrace of pretence. He speaks woe and hypocrisy and blindness and He talks about the seriousness of distorting a system. It's communal, it's not just you and me. Without you realising it, it's contagious and it's spreading. And God in His mercy says, 'Heal the sin-sickness in your soul, because it's affecting the community of which you are part.'

It is a very tough word from Jesus from a passage from which, had I not been allocated my text and subject by the Keswick Council, I doubt I would ever have preached at Keswick. Some of you may be young Christians who haven't met this face of Jesus before. Let me remind you; He is the Gardener with the pruning knife, who with great wisdom moves in on our lives, and out of great love prunes in order that there might be more fruitfulness. He is the Divine Surgeon. He is prepared for amputation, if it brings about the health of the body (Matt. 18:7–9). He is the truthful Prophet who comes and says, 'You are the man, and you are the woman, and this is the heart of the matter' (cf 2 Sam. 12:7).

I want to show you from this passage seven things that make Jesus angry. They are the marks of the pretender.

Pretenders shut the door to truth (verse 13)

God's kingdom is the key to history. One day, the kingdoms of this world will become the kingdoms of our God. All human kingdoms are provisional—Mr Yeltsin's kingdom, Mr Mandela's kingdom, Mr Clinton's kingdom, Mr Major's kingdom. They are all provisional kingdoms.

Matthew takes the kingdom of God seriously. Who rules the world? In chapter 28 he tells us that Jesus told His disciples to go into all the world and teach all nations. That was the measure of the mandate. Why not? He's the king! So the king sends everybody out to the whole world. And did you realise that Matthew 2 is a prophecy? As those wise men come and gather round the cradle of Jesus, it's as if the whole world gathers at the cradle. The scribes and Pharisees, when the kingdom broke in through the ministry and preaching of Jesus, didn't take Him seriously. They refused God's offer of grace, they were blind to the signs of the kingdom's presence in their midst. And what's worse, they didn't practise what they preached (verses 3, 13). Those fifty volumes and 6,000 regulations are not the way to get right with God. God comes to pretenders this evening and says, 'Is there any way in which you are shutting the door to God's truth in your community?'

Do you take Jesus seriously in your community, regularly, offering to all men and women, boys and girls and young people, God's offer of grace? Do you look for the signs of the kingdom, praying them home, praying them with faith, intervening in hope? What about practising what we preach? I have to confess, there have been times in my life when I've baked bread for other people but haven't feasted at the table myself. I've done so because it's much easier to do to just go through the motions.

Lord, if we really want to take seriously what You are saying to us about pretending, help us therefore to ask ourselves the question: do we ever shut the door to Your truth?

Pretenders make clones rather than disciples (verse 15)

The scribes and Pharisees were prepared to travel half way round the world to make a single replica of themselves. Jesus says that the deadly result is their converts become twice as much a son of hell as the scribes and Pharisees, who have substituted what God really wants at all times, in all places; to become like Him—and that had become substituted with 'Become like me', or 'Become like us'.

The more I have reflected on these words the more I have realised their relevance for this word for this church at this time. We hold up our hands and say to the Divine Physician this evening, 'Lord, I am not guilty of pretending, of play-acting.' Have you never said to somebody who has recently become a disciple, 'This is the version to use, and this is the conference to go to, and this is the organisation to give your money to, and this is the proper church to attend . . . we are the pure church'? Whatever happened to Romans 14:5, 'Each one should be fully convinced in his own mind', or Romans 15:5, 'May the God who gives endurance and encouragement give you a spirit of unity among yourselves'—listen!—'as you follow Christ Jesus'? The previous verses have been all about food, regulations and holy days, and all the things that were splitting a church community in Rome down the middle. They were following leaders. I've actually been asked, 'How are you going to vote on this issue, Pastor? I want to know how I should vote.'

The other thing that people have sometimes said to me is, 'Pastor, I wouldn't do it for anybody else, but I'll do it for you.' Then I know that I've got a follower but Jesus hasn't got a disciple.

Pretenders evade promise-keeping (verse 16)

For how many pastors, I wonder, is their opinion formed by the last conversation they had—like the Texan politician who, challenged as to where he stood on a sensitive issue, declared, 'I am on the side of my friends'? In verses 16–22, we see that oaths and promises were part of the system at the time of Jesus' ministry. The scribes and Pharisees had put in an elaborate system together, but it betrayed some cynical attitudes. They'd put escape clauses in, rather as children today might say of a promise, 'It doesn't count—I had my fingers crossed.' They had something far more holy and ceremonial, but their wording enabled them to evade keeping promises.

Oaths and promises were important. John the Baptist was beheaded because of an oath. A king had said to a dancer, 'I'll give you on my oath whatever you ask.' She talked to her mother then demanded, 'I want the head of John the Baptist.' So serious is oath-taking in the day of Jesus, that John the Baptist lost his head (cf Matt. 14:1–12). And it was because of an oath that Peter wept bitterly: with an oath he said, three times, 'I don't know the man' (cf Matt. 26:69–75.)

Jesus comes and breaks into this evil system. He comes and speaks to us this evening about evading promise-keeping. Have you ever had said to you—Sunday-school teacher, youth leader, church administrator, pastoral visitor—'But you promised me.' And back comes the response, 'But I really promised this other person.' It seems so trivial, doesn't it? If it weren't in God's word I'd apologise for raising it here this evening. But it is in God's word, and it comes from the lips of Jesus, in this context of pretending. It has to do with hypocrisy, with this sickness that He wants to heal in us. He wants to make us well, He wants us to take that medicine of repentance.

P. T. Forsyth, the Congregationalist theologian, said, 'If within you there is nothing over you, then you will succumb to what is around you.'

Pretenders major on the minors (verse 23)

Jesus now takes us into the kitchen garden, where herbs like mint, dill and cumin grow. He takes us further, into kitchen preparation. People are meticulous about these tiny little herbs—tithing them, because they want to keep those 6,000 regulations that please God so much. Then we are taken to the preparation of wine, which has to be filtered through gauze so that tiny mosquito gnats are filtered out. And He says, 'The gnat-sized sins are filtered out, but then camel-sized sins are swallowed whole.'

He tells us what they are. 'You have neglected the more important matters of the law–justice, mercy and faithfulness.' It's straight out of Micah:

> And what does the LORD require of you?
> To act justly and to love mercy
> and to walk humbly with your God. (Mic. 6:9)

Notice that God wants both. 'You should have practised the latter, without neglecting the former.' He wants us to sometimes major on minor things, but He also wants us to major on the major things. He wants that wholeness of life.

In 1916 at this very Convention, Graham Scroggie, speaking during a two-year-old war and doubtless with bereaved families present, said, 'The war has widened our horizons and increased our sympathies; and is leading us not to a new message, but to a proper adjustment of the old message to the new condition of things.' Today, in 1996, I wonder whether those words of

Graham Scroggie apply to the kind of situation in which we find ourselves in 1990s United Kingdom. We don't want a new message, but we want a proper adjustment of the old message to the new condition of things.

Last year I went to a very well-known city, by invitation of a very well-known church, to take what was called a 'home mission weekend'. They wanted to focus on the nation, to ask, 'What has God's word to say to the nation today? And what is God's church to do about the state of the nation?' When I met with the planning committee, they said, 'We think you ought to know that in our church, home mission is a Cinderella. All the romance is given to overseas mission.' They were based in a city where there were people dying every week from drugs; there were child prostitutes on the streets; there were homeless people; no doubt there were people with learning disabilities. That was a church, like many churches, that needed to have engraved on all its exit doors, 'You are now entering the mission field.'

It's not somewhere over there, it's somewhere just out here. And God comes this evening and says, 'You can be meticulous about the church programme. Your church notice-board can be tithed so meticulously, to announce all the things that you're doing—prayer meetings, Bible studies, sermons—and yet you can be blind to those greater issues which are to do with justice and mercy and walking faithfully with your God.'

Pretenders concentrate on externals (verse 25)

This is all about cups and saucers.

It's another elaborate scheme. You could have a flat plate without a rim if you were a scribe or a Pharisee. If you touched it, it wouldn't make you unclean. You could have a door knob; and if you touched it, it wouldn't make you unclean. But if you had a plate made of wood and metal—well then, if you touched the wood part that would make you unclean, but not the metal part. The only way you could make some cups and saucers clean was to break them! I'm going to remember that next time I drop the Royal Doulton at home.

Why does Jesus speak about blindness in these verses? Is He

perhaps linking His words about greed and self-indulgence in verse 25 with the sin of gluttony? It might be the sin of eating without saying Grace; it might be the sin of having plenty and hungry people in that particular town going without. I'm not saying that externals—what clothes people wear in church, whether women wear make-up, whether Christians take Sunday newspapers, whether children should watch *Top of the Pops*—are unimportant. But you can get all that right and still not have a pure church.

I have to say, as one who has been nowhere else except the evangelical family—I owe so much to this tribe, to this Convention—that sometimes we have majored on these minor things and concentrated on externals. If we and our churches are still doing that, let's hear what Jesus says through His word.

Paul's letter to the Galatians, that great book about freedom, is a book about add-ons, the add-ons that we add every generation. In Paul's day there was a long list of add-ons; defining who you ate with, what you did to your body, and how you observed certain festivals. We may have done away with Paul's list, but add-ons are still around. Jesus comes and says, 'Watch out; because they can be the mark of the pretender, who concentrates on the externals.'

Pretenders conceal inward death (verse 27)

As the thousands of pilgrims made their way up to the Holy City they would see the recently white-washed tombs plastered with lime, standing out, glistening in the sun. Why were they white-washed? Because if you happened to touch one of the tombs on your way to the great festival, you had to turn round and go back again. Some people had travelled for hours, maybe days. So they made tombs deliberately conspicuous to say, 'Stay away, don't touch, watch out—dead man's bones.'

Jesus takes this picture, it's a dreadful irony. 'I want you to steer clear of these people, because however well-decorated these tombs are, with their tassels and their Scripture-scrolls on their forehead and on their arms; the way people greet them, the titles they bear—I want you to know that they are just dead men's bones.'

I wish that Jesus were only talking about Pharisees. But His word is His word to us this evening. Is it possible that Jesus exposes in us this sixth mark of the pretender, which we have concealed? We are at Keswick, so we must be all right! We carry a title, we carry a Bible, we lead a fellowship, we've been a Christian on the road for so many years! But when you've died inwardly, you know it. There's no passion for mission. There's no feeling for the lost. There's no compulsion to pray. There's no desire to think through the great issues of the day. There's no heart for mercy. And there's no willingness to change.

Listen, sister or brother. There's only one answer to a condition like that, and that is to hear the One who says, 'I am the resurrection and I am the life.' Jesus wants to come and say, 'Even in the dead bones of a marriage, I can come and say I am the resurrection and the life.' Some of you are leading organisations, and you don't just need to hear the words 'I am the resurrection and the life', you need a Lazarus-type resurrection for that organisation. You need to bring Him to the grave, to ask people to take the stone away; and to stagger out as Lazarus and let Jesus say the word to you that will bring you to life again.

Do you know that great line in the hymn, 'Rescue the perishing'?

> Touched by a loving hand, wakened by kindness
> Chords that were broken will vibrate once more.
> *(Fanny. J. Crosby)*

That's the promise of grace, to dead men's bones living in highly decorated Christian tombs this evening. Go for it!

Pretenders abuse God's messengers (verse 29)

It's a murderous record. Here they are on the Memorial Committee for building big statues for prophets long dead. They are very proud of that. It was probably a very prestigious committee.

But Jesus comes and nails it. When they say, 'If we had been there it wouldn't have happened,' he retorts, 'Yes it would.' The A to Z from Abel to Zechariah—Chronicles was the last book in the Hebrew Bible, which is why Zechariah is mentioned in that context: read about the sad death of that prophet of God, where the king connives with others that he should be struck down dead in the very courts of the temple. His dying words were 2 Chronicles 24:22, 'May the LORD see this and call you to account.'

Jesus comes and says, 'Oh, you have filled up your quota.' This is generational sin. See the catalogue of people in verse 34: there had been prophets, wise men and teachers, and what had happened to them? They had been murdered, mugged and harassed. And this was a generational attitude. Verse 36, 'I tell you the truth, all this will come upon this generation.'

And Jesus comes and says, 'What about the abuse of my messengers?'

I want you to know that there are sinful pastors, lazy pastors, inept pastors; and they deserve the discipline of God's family. But I want you to know from the ministry that I am involved in, I meet a lot of sad and discouraged pastors, and they are God's messengers, they are godly messengers, and they are seeking to faithfully bring God's word. It may be that age isn't on their side. Who stood alongside Timothy, and who got alongside Aquila and Priscilla, and who was it who encouraged the four daughters of Philip? And I want to know in this day and age, if, pastor, you've got a new heart for your people as you spend these days as Keswick, have you as God's people, got a new heart to support God's messengers, to recognise them, to honour them, to pray for them, to support them, and to love them?

As we move towards the end of the word, we need to be saying to ourselves, 'Lord is any or part of this true of me, of our community? Is this as You see us now, or sometimes?'

Look at the loving appeal in verse 37, from Christ; the reiterated name, 'O Jerusalem, Jerusalem'. I hear Him say it over my life sometimes: 'O David, David.' He says it over your life: 'O Keith, Keith . . . O Maureen, Maureen . . . O Sylvia, Sylvia . . . O Philip, Philip.' I use those names because they are those of close colleagues, not because I know your name. But if God uses that in order to speak to you out of His loving concern . . .

What does He want to do with you?

That wonderful mother-hen imagery! It is the imagery of Psalm 17:8: 'Keep me as the apple of your eye; hide me in the shadow of your wings.' There's a song based on the same theme: 'Living under the shadow of Your wings, I find security.' That's His longing. 'I long to gather you under the shadow of my wings, that you might find security there.'

But there's a final, dreadful warning. Verse 38: 'Look, your house is left to you desolate'—our house, Lord? We thought it was your house. No longer, friends. This is goodbye time. You want the vineyard? You have the vineyard. You want the temple? You have the temple. You want the house? You have the house. You want the life? You have the life. You want to rule? You rule.

'But Lord, where else can I go, to whom else can I go, who else has the words of eternal life?'

And Jesus comes and says, 'O Jerusalem, Jerusalem', with that word of grace in verse 39. There is hope, there is hope here this evening.

The 'woes' of Matthew 23 are linked with the 'blesseds' of Matthew 5. This is 'woe'; but part of the medicine is to come back and remember the 'blesseds'. Blessed are the poor in spirit, who know they've got nothing! They feel as though they are dressed in filthy rags and they want to stand before the Divine Physician and say, 'I am sick. I didn't realise I was that sick, but I'm sick.' And blessed are those who mourn for their condition. And blessed are those who are meek, the ones who are willing for Jesus to take off the mask and remove years of make-up, in order that the real you might suddenly step forth into the light; no longer learning lines, no longer playing a part but being the person that God intended you to be. And blessed are the real, who say, 'I don't see—and what's worse, I'm leading'—the blind leading the blind.

And Jesus comes and says, 'What do you want Me to do for you?' You know the answer? 'Lord, I want to see so that I might lead others.'

A little boy picked a tulip. It was still a bud, so he began to open it by pulling off the petals. Soon he said to his mother, 'Why is it, that whenever I open a tulip it's a mess, but whenever God opens one, it is beautiful?' His mother was impressed by his insight, but he hadn't finished yet. He added, 'I think I know the reason. The reason is that when God opens a flower, He opens it from the inside.'

God has brought you here this evening to hear afresh about the love of God who has not abandoned you or your community, about the blood of Christ which is available to those who say, 'I am sick,' and about the power of the Holy Spirit to come and indwell and empower that life of yours which has been so prone sin-sickness.

Lord, we are here as sinners; and we want Your cure.

'Change for the Better'

by Rev. Colin Sinclair

2 Corinthians 3:17

Why is it, when somebody meets us after a long time and says, 'You haven't changed a bit', we often feel relieved rather than disappointed? If we understand the gospel of Paul and believe that God has begun a good work in us, that He will bring to conclusion in the day of Jesus Christ, then we will long that day by day, God should be changing us from the inside out.

Freedom

'Now the Lord is the Spirit, and where the Spirit is, there is freedom.'

I suppose 'freedom' is one of the most intoxicating words of the twentieth century. It has a heady sound, it finds an echo within the human heart. It is a fundamental longing for which people will march, sing and fight. The world cries out and demands freedom—freedom from want, from ignorance, from poverty, from disease. And in a generation where we are far quicker to talk about rights than about responsibilities, people have used that word time and again to argue for almost any course of action or any belief. They justify what they are doing as freedom of speech, choice, or political action. Remember *Alice in Wonderland*? A word can mean whatever you want it to mean. But that's not true when we handle God's word. We must handle it all faithfully and properly, in context, and not be satisfied with a nice feeling.

In the last twenty-five years, how many nations have found

that political freedom does not mean economic freedom, and that there are other less visible chains that can bind a people even tighter? Edmund Burke said, 'The price of freedom is eternal vigilance'.

Yesterday our family went to Ambleside where my wife and I spent two nights of our honeymoon. We wanted to show our children the hotel. We found it easily enough, but it's totally changed; it's now a time-share and a bar. Our prospect of afternoon tea and nostalgia disappeared. We thought we knew what our honeymoon hotel was, but now it was a faceless building without memories. The journey had been made to no real purpose.

Sometimes people think that they've got a hold of the Christian life and of their Christian experience; they can name and date it. But when they go back, somehow things have changed and they are in a foreign country. They're like a child in a garden, mesmerised by a colourful butterfly. They reach out and seize it, but when they open their hand all there is a drop of blood and crushed wings.

The freedom that is ours in Christ must never be taken for granted.

Sir Winston Churchill gave Volume 5 of his *History of the Second World War* the subtitle, *How the great democracies triumphed and thus were able to resume the follies which so nearly cost them their lives*. Some cannot see freedom other than as a licence to be answerable to no-one. It's independence, it is autonomy.

One of the biggest difficulties I face working among young people is finding contemporary role-models of commitment, in a world of disposable relationships, a highly mobile society where people do not put roots down in their community, where when you examine marriage closely you find that some enter it with their only commitment being 'to be true to themselves'. How hard it is to explain what commitment means, and illustrate it with examples that relate to the world of young people! And this kind of freedom becomes in the end a glorification of our own choices and desires—the incessant contemporary search to find ourselves, to look back into our past, to understand ourselves—in the name of freedom.

But true freedom is never the freedom to do what I like; that's the worst kind of slavery. Many people just want to be free from God, so they simply discard Him from their thoughts; but real freedom is not to be free from the restraint of others or from God, but to be free from yourself. And Christ came to bring freedom from self in all its forms. Not just freedom from sin, but freedom from our law-keeping, self-justifying mentality that leads to self-righteousness or (if we are honest) to despair. Christian freedom is not just freedom *from*, it is freedom *for*— free to be what God wants me to be and to do what God wants me to do, knowing that His service is perfect freedom.

Christ comes through His word and by His Spirit to set us free to be good—for we are already free to be bad. He sets us free to be saints—for we have already exercised our freedom to be sinners. And when Christ sets you free, He means you to keep that freedom, not to go back into chains and lose your birth-right.

In Scotland we have a range of 3,000-foot mountains called the Munroes. There are people who call themselves 'Munroe Baggers'; they take every opportunity of climbing them. I've done some hill-walking myself. I much enjoy ridge-walking, along ridges such as Striding Edge here in the Lakes. It can be very spectacular as the path gets narrower, and you see on each side deep dark corries, and you hope that the wind won't blow you away as you make your way across the ridge.

The path of Christian freedom is like ridge-walking. There are dangers on either side; the enemies of liberty, of Christian freedom. On one side is licence, but we end up in bondage to our old sinful nature, to the flesh, to self. And on the other side is legalism, which is bondage to law-keeping. And the middle way is the way of liberty, which is freedom in the Spirit.

Which is the greater danger—legalism? Or licence? Of the two, I think the New Testament would emphasise legalism, because it is so deceptive. Unless, of course, you have had experience of legalism, in which case you may well over-compensate and fall down the other side into licence. And I wonder if in a gathering like this, where our theme is clean hands and our desire is to walk holy before our God, one of the greatest temptations by which we might lose our freedom is legalism?

That was why Paul wrote Galatians, that great Magna Carta of Christian freedom, and warned about another gospel.

Legalism—a case history

People can become enslaved out of genuine desire to know and love Christ. Over twenty years ago, I was on the Scripture Union staff in Zambia. Among the students with whom I had contact was a group of fine Christian men who were zealous to see the gospel spread. Disappointed by what seemed to them a lack-lustre, nominal church and by fellow-students whose faith was being compromised because they were at university, they recognised the need for more effort and vigilance. What was causing their contemporaries to drift away? They decided the cause was departure from the truth and Christian lifestyle. 'This is a serious business,' they said. 'It requires earnestness, if we are to be holy to the Lord.'

About a year later, I was asked to give the Bible readings at a national conference of student Christian Unions. The chairman of the first session was a lovely radiant Christian man. But at the second session he said, 'I am sorry, some have rebuked me for smiling during the introduction to the opening session. Such flippancy, they say, is holding us back in doing business with God. I ask your forgiveness.' And laughter went out of many lives.

Soon afterwards, love went too. This group, genuinely wanting to know the Lord, found themselves building walls to protect themselves and those young in the faith, to protect them from going too near the edge. But the problem with building walls is that they have to be visible. Soon we focus on externals—what people do, where they go, what they wear. And we make sure we are inside, which feeds our self-righteousness.

They built their walls for the best of reasons, but they found that others were outside the walls. As they congratulated them-selves, they condemned other people, just as many do, tragically building their ministry on their criticism of others. Their desire was right, but within them something had died. They began to look to the walls and not to the Lord, to listen to the words of their leaders rather than to that of the living God. Laughter went; love went; evangelism went. In the end, as has happened before in church history when legalism reigns, some dried up; and others, dead inside, gave up. The whole thing fell apart when some of the leaders fell into sexual sin. Praise God, some others found freedom and escaped from bondage.

If we are talking about Christian freedom we need to keep our eyes closely on the Lord. Legalistic ministry can say 'Do this' and 'Do that', but it can't give us the power to obey. Even if we do obey, it's not from the heart, and we are in a worse situation than before. It's like the little girl who was told to stand up in class. She was heard to mutter, 'I might be standing up on the outside, but on the inside I'm still sitting down.'

Some major in rules and regulations. Some are kept under a dark cloud of guilt, and in so doing kill joy, power and effective witness for Christ. The tragedy is that some people can't feel spiritual unless they are carrying a weight of guilt. Is not the Christ who set us free the Christ who died for us on the cross? Legalism leaves people immature, for they are not encouraged to think for themselves. It leaves them guilty and afraid. They spend a lot of time on externals and miss the heart of the matter.

Some people have their religion beautifully packaged, attractively wrapped, and tied up with a ribbon and a big bow. But inside, the box is empty. There's nothing there.

The way forward

Sadly, some New Testament churches can have an Old Testament ministry. That is what Paul is talking about, as he compares the glories of the new covenant to the old religion, and shows us the way forward.

The contrast between stone and flesh (verse 2)
The old religion was written in Ten Commandments on stone, chipped out in granite over forty days. The new religion is to be written on hearts. It's softer material, but it still takes time to

write in human hearts; you need to be more tender. It's a change from an outward religion to an inward one. It's easy to paint the Ten Commandments on a church wall—much harder to try and write them on the heart. But Jesus cares not about externals, but what is inside. It is what is on the inside that makes someone dirty: pride, jealousy, lust, covetousness. We need a new heart.

The contrast between letter and Spirit (verse 6)

It's a change from letter to spirit. We have heard from Stuart Briscoe some of the ways in which people, fearful from breaking the law, began to codify it. The Sabbath, classified under thirty-nine headings, each with thirty nine sub-heads—don't let a woman look in a mirror on the Sabbath, because if she sees a grey hair she cannot resist plucking it out, and that's harvesting. Don't let that old man use his stick to prop himself along to the synagogue, in case he drags it in the dust, and that's ploughing.

No wonder Jesus said, 'Come to me, all you who are weary and burdened, and I will give you rest' (Matt. 11:28). Is there anybody here tonight who is weary from trying to keep the empty box in place, who needs to come to Christ for new life and freedom? Jesus came to make the complicated simple, to take the Ten Commandments and summarise them in the two great words: love God and love your neighbour. The gospel does not demand of us 'Give, give, give,' but talks about the gifts that God has given, the gift of His Son to be our Saviour and the gift of His Spirit in our hearts.

The contrast between death and life (verse 7)

One of the frightening things about goodness is that is so off-putting, 'Lord, make the bad people good and then make the good people nice.' We often skip over, in the Parable of the Prodigal Son which is really the Parable of Two Lost Sons, the sting in the tail—the drab, dreary story of the elder brother: 'You never gave me a kid.' No wonder, he would never have had a party! I can't help asking, why did the younger brother go to the far country? Perhaps because the last thing he wanted to become was like his older brother. And did he stay away so long because the last thing he could face was the sneer in his brother's face if he returned? God forgive us if, by our failure to show joy and love of Christ, we've driven someone into the far country, and if by our unwillingness to accept and forgive we delay their return.

The contrast between a fading glory and a lasting glory (verses 10–11)

The law and the gospel came from God. Moses and Christ were sent by God, and God chose to send His Spirit on the church on the very day that the Children of Israel gave thanks for the law on the Day of Pentecost. That law was given by God to Moses; when he came down the mountain his face was shining bright, because he had been in the presence of God. But as he descended the radiance began to dim. He put a veil over his face as the glory began to fade.

But the phosphorescence of the new covenant can be upon your life all the time, shining out from within as a moral radiance that transforms the inner character of people, penetrating beneath the surface to the heart. It's not a superficial shine on the face, but the very image of God embossed on human character; a glory that will never fade but will go on deepening as long as time shall last and into eternity.

Paul also uses the picture of a veil in a second way, as a picture of the blindness that developed so that people could not see the truth of God in Christ

Finding liberty

If the danger is licence on one hand and legalism on the other, how do we find liberty? Verse 16, 'But whenever anyone turns to the Lord, the veil is taken away.' 'Oh,' they say to the vicar, 'I see now, it's so clear! Why didn't I see that before?'

It begins as we turn to the Lord Jesus Christ and see Him as He is, the only Saviour and the supreme Lord.

The Spirit's work in freedom

We come to our text: 'Now the Lord is the Spirit, and where the Spirit of the Lord is, there is freedom.' The gift of the risen and ascended Christ is the gift of His Holy Spirit for all Christians.

The converse is Romans 8:9—'If anyone does not have the Spirit of Christ, he does not belong to Christ.' I wonder , in our experience-hungry times, whether we need to ask, not: 'How can I have more of God?' But: 'How can God have more of me? . . . Do I quench the Holy Spirit? Do I lie to the Holy Spirit by pretending more than is true of my experience? Do I grieve the Holy Spirit in the way that I live?'

The Spirit is Christ's gift to His church to lead us into all the truth, to hold us together, to enable us to make Christ known, to glorify Jesus. And the Spirit applies in us what Christ has accomplished for us, by His death and resurrection. So our lives are not to be controlled by laws (which is legalism), nor by lust (which is licence), but by love, which is the way of the Spirit. Going back onto our mountain top, walking along the ridge, we are to walk in freedom, striding along in faith in Christ, breathing in the Spirit of God and experiencing the sunshine and invigorating presence of God's love and grace.

Peace with God

For Paul, freedom meant first of all recognising the Lord and submission to Him, desiring His will, not his own. It began with a relationship to God, not by being solitary. It involved interdependence, not independence. As John Stott says, 'True freedom is freedom from my silly little self in order to live responsibly in love to God and to others.' The person who is truly free trusts, loves and obeys God through Christ. And in the Spirit, love then serves others and lives before God with a clear conscience, growing in holiness and love.

Christian freedom is not freedom to indulge our flesh but to crucify it, so that we will not exploit our neighbour but serve him; we will not disregard the law but fulfil it in love. That freedom is found when we find peace with God; the cleansing of our guilty conscience through faith in Christ crucified, the unutterable joy of forgiveness, acceptance, access and sonship; and the experience of mercy without merit.

As we are transformed into the likeness of Christ we become increasingly free. When people turn to Him, the scales fall off their eyes by the work of the Spirit. The chains that they were held by are broken. They are brought into the glorious liberty of the children of God, from death to life, from condemnation to righteousness:

> My chains fell off, my heart was free;
> I rose, went forth, and followed Thee.
> (*Charles Wesley*)

Who would be satisfied with a candlelit, formal, trying–to–be good religion, when you can open your mind, heart and will to the glorious changing and transforming surge of Christ Himself, living in our hearts by the Holy Spirit? The fact of the Spirit, life-giving and enabling, is the glory of the gospel which we too easily forget. When we do we lapse back into a dreadful bondage to struggle, it isn't what God desires.

Exhortations and commands to holiness can sometimes crush and bring emotional desolation. But to be told that the power and the life of the risen Christ have been given to you and are for you to use is gospel news. It speaks of glorious freedom and hope. We are set free by the Spirit, when we receive Christ as our Saviour and Lord. And as we look at that Christ and at His glory, we are being transformed.

The power at work in us
Verse 18 uses a word from nature to describe a caterpillar turning into a butterfly. That transforming power can be at work in us. You see it in the transparent integrity of Christ on the Mountain of Transfiguration; and Paul speaks of that transformation by 'the renewal of your minds' (Romans 12:2). God is in the process of doing this as we behold Jesus.

It's said you become like the people that you gaze upon. A long-married husband and wife can grow to resemble each other. You can see it in adopted children as they grow to resemble their new parents. It's even said of pets and their owners. People who hero-worship film-stars, athletes or musicians copy their dress, manner and style.

So, too, you become like Jesus as you meditate on His words, as you use the means of grace that allows us to come close to God—word and Spirit working together in perfect harmony, without any contradiction. The great joy of the Spirit of God is that He is a self-effacing member of the Trinity. His is a searchlight ministry, which points away from self and points to Jesus, and delights to magnify the Lord in our midst.

Looking at Jesus

The degree to which we reflect Jesus depends on the time we spend looking at Him. Are you are a glancer, or a gazer? We are to gaze long and often. James uses a very simple illustration of the law of liberty: he talks of someone glancing in a mirror and forgetting what he sees (Jas. 1:23–25). We glance at the mirror to straighten our tie, to comb our hair—but we don't look long. But as we gaze into God's word which was prompted by the Spirit of God, and through which we get understanding by the Spirit of God, so we see Jesus.

I have to say, I am increasingly concerned by the little my generation and the one before it within the evangelical church know of the Scriptures, compared to how well those who are older than I do. The Spirit uses that word to etch Christ into our character. If it's true that Christians read their Bible, then the world reads Christians. If we are not reading our Bibles, then what on earth does the world see in our own lives?

Freedom in the early church

Finally, let me look with you as we end, at the experience of this freedom in the life of the early church. If I look in the Acts of the Apostles I see several results when the Spirit came upon the people of God.

First, it seems to me *there was a new quality to them*. They were lifted to a higher plane and they fulfilled their potential. Thus it is that a parlour maid can become a Gladys Aylward; a girl frightened to cross the street can become a Mary Slessor of Calabar; a cobbler can become a William Carey; and others of us can say, 'We never realised that God could take me and give and develop gifts that were all to His glory.'

The second thing I notice is, *they were set free*. They were released from all prejudices. They found themselves increasingly able to understand others in a new way, to get inside their thought-world and heart-world and resonate with them; and then clearly, in a way they could understand, to present the gospel faithfully to them. The great wonder is that the gospel has gone, and is going, to all cultures. In each place it rings true, as people who have been set free by the Spirit come to understand the people that they have come to serve in Christ. And they stop seeing people at a distance, through distorted lenses, but see them close up.

Thirdly, *they used their new freedom with amazing courage.* They believed that God was with them, so they were not afraid to speak for Christ. They believed He would give them wisdom when they faced challenges so they were neither paralysed nor fossilised by problems, but were transformed and transforming in them.

And fourthly, *they were set free by the Spirit, to a new life of holiness,* as the fruit of the Spirit began to shine out from them. We believe Christians grow not like Christmas trees, but like fruit trees. We decorate our Christmas trees with bright artificial decorations. But the fruit is real, it lasts; and it's not a mystical fruit, it's a moral fruit.

If you look at people boating on the Lakes, you'll notice that those in rowing boats face backwards, and those in sailing dinghies face forwards. In a rowing boat all you can hope in is your own effort; you struggle away. But in a sailing dinghy, the wind fills the sails and you move forwards and on into the direction you were meant to go.

Is yours a rowing-boat faith, or a sailing-dinghy faith?

Is your life facing backwards, all effort, unsure if you're ever going to win against the tide?

Or do you have the freedom that is found 'where the Spirit of the Lord is'?

KESWICK 1996
TAPES, VIDEOS AND BOOKS

Catalogues and price lists of audio tapes of the Keswick Convention platform ministry, including much not included in the present book, can be obtained from:

ICC (International Christian Communications)
Silverdale Road
Eastbourne
East Sussex BN20 7AB.

Details of videos of selected sessions can be obtained from:

Mr Dave Armstrong
STV Videos
Box 299
Bromley, Kent BR2 9XB.

Some previous annual Keswick volumes (all published by STL/OM) are still in print, and can be ordered from your local Christian bookseller or direct from the publishers, OM Publishing, STL Ltd, P O Box 300, Carlisle, Cumbria CA3 0QS, England UK.

KESWICK 1997

The annual Keswick Convention takes place each July at the heart of England's beautiful Lake District. The two separate weeks of the Convention offer an unparalleled opportunity for listening to gifted Bible exposition, experiencing Christian fellowship with believers from all over the world, and enjoying something of the unspoilt grandeur of God's creation.

Each of the two weeks has a series of five morning Bible Readings, followed by other addresses throughout the rest of the day. The programme in the second week is a little less intensive, and it is often referred to as 'Holiday Week'. There are also regular meetings throughout the fortnight for young people, and a Children's Holiday Club.

The dates for the 1997 Keswick Convention are 12–19 July (Convention Week) and 19–26 July (Holiday Week). The Bible Reading speakers are Bishop Michael Baughen and Mr Charles Price respectively. Other speakers during the fortnight include Rev. Mark Ashton, Rev. Clive Calver, Rev. Liam Goligher, Rev. Steve Gaukroger and Rev. Vaughan Roberts.

For further information, write to:

The Administrator
Keswick Convention Centre
Skiddaw Street
Cumbria CA12 4BY
Telephone: 017687 72589